COLORED
SCHOOL CHILDREN IN
NEW YORK

BY

FRANCES BLASCOER

Special Investigator for the Committee on Hygiene of School Children of the Public
Education Association of the City of New York

EDITED BY ELEANOR HOPE JOHNSON

Chairman of the Committee on Hygiene of School Children of the Public Education
Association

NEGRO UNIVERSITIES PRESS
NEW YORK

Originally published in 1915
by Public Education Association
of the City of New York

Reprinted from a copy in the collections
of the Brooklyn Public Library

Reprinted 1970 by
Negro Universities Press
A DIVISION OF GREENWOOD PRESS, INC.
NEW YORK

SBN 8371-2935-4

FOREWORD

In submitting the appended report on colored school children in New York city, I wish to thank those directly or indirectly connected with the investigation or with work among colored people who have by their co-operation aided in gathering the material and preparing it for publication.

I wish to express my feeling of special obligation to Dr. William H. Maxwell, City Superintendent of Schools, for his generous letter of introduction to school officials, and to the principals and teachers who have been particularly concerned in this study. Thanks are due to Miss Kate H. Claghorn of the School of Philanthropy, Dr. Leonard P. Ayres of the Russell Sage Foundation, and Dr. Ira S. Wile of the Board of Education, for criticism and suggestions, to Dr. J. C. Fisk of the Committee on the Hygiene of School Children for examining and treating children in need of medical care; to the officers of the Committee on Hygiene of School Children and to the Director of the Public Education Association, who have given much assistance in constructive work on the report.

Particular expression of gratitude is due to the colored people whose homes I visited and who, almost without exception, evinced a strong desire to aid in arriving at an understanding of the problems under consideration.

FRANCES BLASCOER

January 30, 1915

CONTENTS

LIST OF TABLES

vii

INTRODUCTION

In the year 1911 one of the large public schools of New York city had occasion to report to the school authorities a number of cases of colored children who appeared to be in need of special attention outside as well as in the school. Their classroom difficulties, in the opinions of their teachers, resulted almost entirely from the unsanitary, immoral or wholly neglected conditions in which they were living. Several of these cases were looked up by visitors working from different agencies, and what seemed to be a large percentage of immorality and weakened mentality was found.

At the same time persons interested in the welfare of the colored race, particularly in the children living in crowded city communities, were asking the question, what philanthropic activity would be of most help to these growing children in securing for them a more hopeful future than the present condition of their parents would seem to promise them. Finally, the Public Education Association was asked, through its Committee on the Hygiene of School Children, to conduct an investigation into the living conditions of colored children whose school progress had been retarded for various reasons, and so help in solving these puzzling questions. This Committee has always believed that answers to many problems regarding child-help could be found by making a study from the school as a starting-point, and that agencies for betterment, if focused upon the school life, would make a very natural and constructive connection from that point with the outside life of the child. The Committee gladly took up the work, therefore, and planned to make a study not only of groups of children from the several schools located in neighborhoods thickly settled with colored people, but also of the various welfare agencies which would naturally deal with the different problems as they should be presented in the histories of these children. It was planned that the investigation should consist not only of a collection of facts regarding these children, their homes, and the best methods of bringing about improved conditions for them, but also of following up the cases of children reported as "difficult," and doing any immediate thing which should make for their present as well as their future welfare.

An investigator was appointed who could at the same time do the practical work and so accomplish a three-fold object: secure an immediate betterment of conditions for the children investigated; throw light on individual schoolroom problems for the teachers whose work was being made vastly more difficult by these bad conditions; and secure facts on which could be based definite plans for future improvement. The report is submitted with every wish that it may furnish useful suggestions both to public and private agencies as to how best to deal with the untoward conditions often surrounding this large section of New York's future citizens. The Committee wishes to express most heartily its appreciation of the co-operation given both by public school officials and by those private agencies that have dealt promptly and efficiently with the cases concerning which their help was asked.

Because the Public Education Association believes that many facts of real constructive value can best be gained by studying the lives of school children in the light of their school records it further believes that "following-up" the school histories of such children into their homes and into the streets is one of the most important pieces of work that can be undertaken; that it must be carried on with tact, persistence and thoroughness, and demands in its performance ability and good judgment. If the report seems to criticize various agencies because of what appears to us to be a failure to realize the need or plan sufficiently for the accomplishment of this important piece of work, it is not because we do not appreciate the difficulties in the way but because we feel the point cannot be overemphasized. In Appendix I are given instances of cases where such follow-up work has not been done with completeness. The reasons why it has not been done may have been very good; we have considered only the fact and its results.

Where information was secured or criticism expressed concerning organizations which could be of interest to them only individually, such material has been sent separately to these organizations. Many recommendations have been made regarding separate activities. These have been included in the report when possible, and an effort has been made to group them in the chapter called "Needs and Recommendations."

3

At the beginning of the investigation an effort was made to keep closely to the narrowed subject of the home, community and school needs of colored children, as represented by the groups studied, and to avoid the larger subject of racial questions and difficulties. It was soon found, however, that this was impossible. Individual problems were often inextricably involved in the "Negro problem," and one of the clearest points brought out was the great variety and uncertainty in public opinion and the influence that fact has on individual needs.

One difficulty in dealing with this question seems to be that the tendency has been to study it in sections. Those people who have held most sympathetic relations with colored people as individuals are often hardest upon them as a race. Those leaders who work with enthusiasm in support of equal justice and opportunity for the colored race appear to these less determined upholders of racial equality to overlook the immediate application of this equality and so to refuse to consider the human elements of the problem. The result is an instability in the public attitude which makes it difficult to predict what form public opinion will take next. Meanwhile individuals of the colored race are achieving much, and whole communities of colored people are rising rapidly in education, refinement and ability.

We are constantly learning, through the interpretation by sympathetic students of various races of immigrants, the several ways in which these aliens may contribute to our national life; and each discovery, especially in the different fields of art, is hailed with joy by constructive patriots. Surely it is time for the Negro to be considered in the light of a national asset and his loyalty, patience, sympathetic kindliness and artistic instinct be counted on as real contributions to our national welfare. In this mind, let us discuss the present and future of colored children.*

The report seems to show that with these children, perhaps more than with those of any other race group, their faults are the defects of their virtues. In cultivating the latter, one is at the same moment and by the same means correcting the former. All children are made self-conscious, sullen and finally irresponsible by constantly holding them up to an impossible standard. It is so with the child members, whether or not of mature years,

* The Music School Settlement is making a definite effort in the direction of developing the artistic ability of the colored race and for that reason alone, if for no other, its work is of the utmost importance.

of this child race. To find what standard is possible it is necessary to study many individuals, those who have achieved and those who have not, as well as the racial history of this section of the world's family. More than this, the necessities of their lives here must be studied. The United States is not an ideal nation. We cannot plan for any race relations with an ideal community. These children will in the nature of things meet many difficulties, as will children of the nations coming to us from beyond the seas. Justice for all is not yet the positive, unqualified thing we wish it were and hope it is going to be. New York schools seem to have met more nearly this ideal justice as it concerns the treatment of races, than have the industries or the organized amusements or, possibly, the private charities. We must encourage the schools to continue and to perfect the plan upon which they have been working. Constant pressure must be put on other forces for betterment that they may look upon all who desire to use them with an equal eye.

The report gives few, perhaps no, recommendations that would not apply to the children of other races. Where the application is more true in regard to colored children it seems to be largely because of this lack of equal justice in the cases of their parents. Race weakness appears but this could easily be balanced by the same or similar weakness in other races. Given an education carefully adapted to his needs and a fair chance for employment, the normal child of any race will succeed, unless the burden of wrong home conditions lies too heavily upon him. Any philanthropic effort for the encouragement or improvement of these children, to be successful, must take into account their peculiar virtues—affection, loyalty, home loving spirit—not their defects. It is this conclusion of the report which applies to colored children more than to the children of any other race, and should make them easier rather than harder to help in their climb upwards. Our country has a very real debt to pay and it can be paid only by helping these children to find for themselves the place in our nation which shall contribute most to their own and its best development.

ELEANOR HOPE JOHNSON,
Chairman Committee on Hygiene of School Children.

JANUARY, 1915.

COLORED SCHOOL CHILDREN IN NEW YORK

SCOPE AND METHOD OF INVESTIGATION

Various appeals from the public schools and other agencies for help in solving special problems in cases of delinquent colored children led the Public Education Association to decide to investigate the extent of such problems, find if possible the sources of the difficulties and recommend ways of solution. The hope has been that, on the basis of the findings, recommendations for preventive and constructive work among colored people might be made to public and private agencies so that the future of the children might promise more that is good than exists in the present life of their parents.

The cases which indicated the necessity for this inquiry appeared on a first analysis to show that they were made up of the usual juvenile delinquencies—truancy, sex immorality, stealing, etc.—encountered by all who work with children, and made familiar to the investigator during five years of social work on the lower East Side among Jewish, Italian and Irish children. Attention had also recently been called to like misdemeanors among pupils of public schools in the Bronx, as well as among the colored children of the upper West Side.

This investigation of colored school children, therefore, has concerned itself not alone with the histories of these children, but has endeavored to learn as well whether the same forces are at work with colored children as with those of other groups in causing the difficulties complained of, and whether the same preventive and remedial measures are available and practicable to meet their needs.

The time allotted to making the investigation and writing the report was one year—from December, 1912, to December, 1913.

In order to understand the work of the agencies already engaged in social, civic and material betterment among the colored people, it was decided to make a preliminary survey of the field and interviews were obtained with principals and teachers of schools, agents of organizations, heads of settlements and other activities and pastors of churches and missions. The results of this study are given in the section entitled "Survey of General Conditions" and in Appendix II.

It was also decided to obtain from a detailed study of 500 elementary school children facts which should show as fully as possible the way their time was spent both in and outside the school, the nature of their homes and the connection which seemed to exist between bad or good home conditions and school life. The study was to concern itself with as many family conditions —over-crowding, broken homes, economic status, etc.—as the one investigator in the limited time allowed her might find possible.

At the end of a full school year a report was to be presented covering the information obtained in this study, not only concerning the children but also the various social agencies which are or which might be employed in their betterment.

Dr. William H. Maxwell, Superintendent of Schools, provided a letter of introduction to the principals of the schools which facilitated access to school records and authorized principals and teachers to assist in the work of the investigation.

For the purpose of comparing individuals and conditions affecting them and to furnish a check on the results found, it was planned to study a group of normal school children in the grammar grades of certain selected schools and to contrast with them the children who were referred to the investigator by principals and teachers as troublesome, or for other reasons. The latter group did not, however, include all the troublesome colored children dealt with through the public schools during the period covered by the investigation. The National League on Urban Conditions Among Negroes had appointed two school visitors before this investigation was undertaken, and the Society for the Prevention of Cruelty to Children had, through the Children's Court, placed on probation or committed for improper guardianship and for juvenile delinquencies, other colored children.

Close co-operation was maintained with these agencies through-out the investigation. The card for recording the information secured in the course of the investigation was made by Mr. Earle Clark, statistician of the Russell Sage Foundation, from an outline that had been formulated as a basis for the investigation and report.

First consideration was given to those elementary school children specially referred to the investigator by principals or teachers. The details involved in many of the cases, as well as the short time in which the children were available for inter-viewing, made it possible to include only 441 elementary school pupils in the investigation instead of the 500 originally contem-plated. It was early felt, however, that a study of the colored boys and girls attending high and trade schools might help to clarify tendencies and vocational problems, and a group of 15 high school boys and 37 high school girls and 38 Manhattan Trade School girls were included, bringing the total number of children studied up to 531.

Of the 441 elementary school children making up the body of the investigation, 53 were specially reported by principals and teachers. The remaining 388 were boys and girls in the Chil-dren's Aid Society School for colored children, and in Public Schools 28, 69, 89, 100, 119, and 141, three being uptown and three downtown schools, covering the colored districts between 34th and 42nd Streets, on San Juan Hill (59th to 65th Streets), and in Harlem.

The children could be seen only after school and on Saturday and Sunday, and even then there was no certainty that they would be found at home. It was necessary to limit the number of visits devoted to finding any one child to three, and in the majority of cases that number of calls was needed before finding any of the family at home.

Much evening time and many Sundays were spent in visiting homes, when for special reasons it was necessary to consult parents who were at work during the day, or who were at home only once a week.

The children were estimated by the teachers' judgment of their mentality and character in addition to the findings of the investigator as well as by their class marks. After about twenty-five had been studied a considerable discrepancy developed between the two estimates, and the former was more in harmony than the latter with a careful study of the child in his home and street relations.*   In a number of instances, however, both class marks and teachers' estimates were modified by conditions not previously known to the teacher; as, for instance, in the cases of three girls rated as "lazy and undependable," each of whom after several visits was found to be suffering acutely from malaria. One girl was receiving dispensary treatment twice a week for this ailment; a second was not only suffering from malaria but had a history of diphtheria, scarlet fever, typhoid and pneumonia; while the third had only recently come from the south, her family having removed to New York because every member had become infected with malaria while living in a low, swampy district.

The estimate of living conditions was based on the following considerations: first, on whether both parents were living, and living at home; whether both were intelligent and sober, and whether the mother remained at home during the day to care for the children; whether the home was clean and light; and whether the number of persons in the household were prorated properly to the number of rooms occupied.

As the investigation progressed, it was found that the out-of-school development and amusement coincided, almost without exception, to the quality of home life indicated by the conditions enumerated above.

Statements concerning earnings and occupations of family members are based on information received from those members. In a number of instances, as for example in the case of railway employees where there is a standard wage for given occupations, and also in cases of a number of employees of business firms, confirmation was secured from employers with no resulting discrepancies.

On visiting the homes the purpose of the investigation was fully explained and the co-operation of the family sought for the purpose of arriving at a true understanding of conditions and methods of bettering them.   There was a general expression of interest by parents and much warm appreciation of the fact that the inquiry had been undertaken.   Concerning family incomes, however, there was considerable hesitation in giving definite information and this matter was not pressed.   Only three objections have been made to the investigation, one of them coming from an

* See Appendix I.

immoral woman from whose custody it was sought to remove her children.

Tenements in all sections of the colored districts were visited freely, although reasonable caution was exercised about going after dark into neighborhoods or houses generally regarded as unsafe. No unpleasantness whatever was encountered.

With regard to school conditions, the investigation did not contemplate any criticism of existing pedagogical methods; it is taken for granted that such shortcomings as may exist react on the colored children as well as on the white ones and that the school records, therefore, undoubtedly reflect those shortcomings. It was, however, necessary to have conferences with principals and teachers on questions of discipline which naturally came up in connection with the cases reported by them of boys and girls presenting unusual problems. Suggestions were made, discussed, and accepted or rejected by the principals, and they appeared to appreciate the more complete understanding of conditions and the coöperation established with agencies having a bearing on them, which the investigation succeeded in bringing about.

With the social agencies, a special effort was made to push as far as possible any question concerning their methods of dealing with their problem where colored people were concerned, as this was the best means that suggested itself of securing a basis for a sound constructive program.

PART I

SURVEY OF GENERAL CONDITIONS

I. Schools

The law of New York State provides that there shall be no separation of races in the schools; and in those districts in which colored pupils have been attending school for years, the principals and teachers apparently have no "color problem" in their minds. The majority of them expressed surprise that there should be any investigation of colored school children, *per se*, and said that, so far as the school is concerned, the colored child presents the same problems as the white child. Those making normal progress they designated as "children of good parents."

On the other hand, in the schools in which the colored population is a new factor (and it is those schools that they are attending in the largest numbers), there is a decided differentiation of the problem of the colored child in the opinion of the principals and teachers, and all manner of questions present themselves as peculiar to colored people, ranging from the effect of street life on colored school children to the belief that the presence of these children had lowered standards of scholarship and conduct in the schools. With one exception, none of these principals or teachers had taught in the schools in which there were large numbers of immigrant children, but had been teaching children of the second or third generation of American born parents of the better grade.

The distribution of colored pupils in the public schools of Manhattan, as reported by principals to whom a questionnaire was sent, is given in Table 1, opposite.

TABLE I.—DISTRIBUTION OF COLORED PUPILS IN THE PUBLIC ELEMENTARY SCHOOLS*

Borough of Manhattan, October, 1913

School No.	Colored			White		
	Boys	Girls	Total	Boys	Girls	Total
3	2	1	3	551	1,434	1,985
5	33	15	48	2,254	694	2,948
6	6	24	30	497	968	1,465
9	3	53	56	212	782	994
10	23	...	23	1,634	....	1,634
11	31	...	31	1,245	....	1,245
14	2	...	2	1,359	1,270	2,629
16	9	...	9	990	23	1,013
17	1	15	16	410	1,285	1,695
18	3	5	8	1,003	288	1,291
24	81	...	81	1,181	....	1,181
26	31	...	31	465	....	465
27	...	1	1	1,053	928	1,981
28	38	104	142	167	861	1,028
29	2	1	3	246	239	485
30	28	27	55	1,103	427	1,530
32	86	50	136	1,139	288	1,427
33	...	13	13	835	1,154	1,989
37	17	...	17	1,317	172	1,489
39	20	...	20	1,453	....	1,453
41	6	32	38	77	1,017	1,094
43	36	24	60	1,339	1,091	2,430
46	26	40	66	1,246	1,179	2,425
47 (deaf)	...	1	1	125	117	242
50	1	1	2	84	1.075	1,159
51	7	9	16	1,251	372	1,623
53	...	18	18	420	1,342	1,762
54	3	4	7	252	1,197	1,449
56	...	30	30	....	1,268	1,268
57	...	5	5	....	....	....
58	46	50	96	756	240	996
59	3	6	9	590	1,574	2,164
67	29	8	37	412	91	503
68	78	163	241	366	954	1,320
69	77	108	185	686	509	1,195
70	33	20	53	1,127	331	1,458
72	...	17	17	....	2,018	2,018
73	5	3	8	607	618	1,225
74	2	1	3	1,400	656	2,056
76	1	4	5	264	1,147	1,411
Model	2	4	6	395	565	960
84	2	23	25	301	959	1,260
89	923	354	1,277	482	82	564
90	25	54	79	756	1,831	2,587

* This table does not include P. S. 87 and P. S. 166 (both boys' schools) whose principals did not co-operate in the investigation.

Other schools omitted in the list reported no colored pupils on their registers.

Colored children constitute a little over 4% of all the pupils in these schools.

TABLE I.—DISTRIBUTION OF COLORED PUPILS IN THE PUBLIC
ELEMENTARY SCHOOLS—(*Continued*)

School No.	Colored			White		
	Boys	Girls	Total	Boys	Girls	Total
93	8	80	88	2,911	1,184	4,095
94	18	49	67	619	993	1,612
95	5	3	8	2,036	532	2,568
100	55	298	353	50	157	207
101	2	2	4	897	1,308	2,205
103	2	3	5	1,325	1,179	2,504
106	...	1	1	456	443	899
107	5	4	9	369	292	661
117	8	6	14	432	359	791
119	56	718	774	289	1,017	1,306
121	13	10	23	957	1,106	2,063
141	41	125	166	383	571	954
151	1	4	5	517	979	1,496
159	...	3	3	459	2,502	2,961
165	9	4	13	1,382	373	1,755
169	2	2	4	85	73	158
170	...	2	2	....	1,348	1,348
171	26	10	36	2,536	646	3,182
179	103	53	156	1,223	372	2,595
184	4	1	5	2,223	1,210	3,433
186	5	4	9	1,376	1,294	2,670
190	1	...	1	178	684	862
Total	2,120	2,702	4,822	55,859	50,334	106,193

Public School 89 on Lenox Avenue, running from 134th to
135th Streets, had the largest registration of colored pupils—1277
out of a total of 1841, the next largest being Public School 119,
a girls' school on 133rd Street near Eighth Avenue, which had
774 colored girls out of a total of 2080 pupils. Public School
100, at 135th Street and Fifth Avenue, had a large proportion of
colored pupils, but was in process of dismemberment during
the year of the investigation because of the growing demand for
space by the Vocational School for Boys, which, with the Wadleigh High School Annex (for girls), occupied the same building.

Public School 68, at 112 West 128th Street, with 241 colored
boys and girls, is the only other Harlem school showing any large
number of colored pupils.

In the downtown districts Public School 141, with 166 colored
pupils, Public School 69 with 185, and Public School 28 with 142,
had the largest proportion of colored pupils in the schools re-

porting. Public School 166, at 89th Street near Columbus Avenue, and Public School 87, at 77th Street and Amsterdam Avenue, both of which have a large number of colored boys, did not coöperate in the investigation, as noted in Table I.

The smaller proportion of colored pupils in the downtown schools is partly accounted for by the fact that the Children's Aid Society conducts a school at 212 West 63rd Street, the Henrietta Industrial School, with a registration of 430 colored pupils from 1A to 4B grades. This school and St. Mark's Parochial School, at 34 West 134th Street, registering about 150 boys and girls, are the only distinctively colored schools in the city.

In order to reach, in this survey of general conditions, a fair estimate of the conditions among school children that were either modified or caused by the fact that some of these children belonged to the colored race, and of the general conditions in the schools particularly affecting these colored children, the different principals and teachers in the schools having the largest percentage of colored pupils were interviewed. The results of these interviews are here summarized.

The first question that arose was why two schools purely for colored children were maintained, even though these are private or corporate schools, when New York's policy is opposed to segregation in the schools. One principal believed that none of the public school principals, with possibly one exception, welcomed colored children. Another said that colored children were obliged, because of their color, to associate with an inferior class of white children in the public schools, and that their naturally good manners were spoiled by this association. Many of the children had even complained to her that they had been called "nigger" by both teachers and pupils in the public schools. For this reason a separate school was presumably welcomed by them. On the other hand, one of the principals interviewed said the colored children were noticeably bad-tempered in school, attacking each other on slight provocation; that they were intractable; and that the class spirit among these children was bad. In this school noticeable prejudice was evident on the part of some of the teachers towards the parents of the colored children and a certain feeling against the children themselves. This subject was taken up later on in the investigation by the district superintendent, and the feeling or its manifestation greatly changed. One head of department spoke of threats made against her by parents of colored girls she had disciplined. As a partial explanation of this it was discovered that she was accustomed to use sarcasm freely in disciplining her pupils, most of whom were adolescents. One of the girls became so exasperated that she threw an ink-stand at the teacher's head. This girl had an unblemished record of good conduct in another school during the two years subsequent to the incident above referred to.

The principal of another school, where sarcasm had been freely used, said that he would be glad of any suggestions that would help him instil better spirit into the children. Pupil self-government was mentioned, but it was felt that for the present it involved too much outside work from a staff of teachers already taxed to their utmost capacity. No branches of the Public Schools Athletic League or other social activities had been organized in this school.

Still another principal said her chief trial was the attitude of those teachers in her school who, because of their work in the district, thought they "knew all about the colored people," in consequence of which she had forbidden any allusion to color by either teachers or pupils. She said she herself had no trouble whatever in her relations with either parents or children.

A third principal said he thought when colored boys and girls reached the age of about twelve years they became unable to adjust themselves to their environment, and he attributed this inability to their consciousness of a difference between themselves and other children. This principal had received numerous complaints from colored boys that they had been "beaten up" by white boys on their way to school. In another school the situation was reversed, white boys complaining that they had been assaulted by colored boys. Opinion differed as to whether or not this street trouble was serious enough to be termed race riots. The school people were inclined to consider it serious. Social workers and clergymen, however, thought it merely gang spirit, one clergyman deprecating the fact that any serious notice was being taken of it. He said he had found a not-too-strenuous "Now, boys, be off!" sufficient to disperse any gang fights he had seen.

No race feeling was reported among the girls. The only expression having a bearing on their relations came from a downtown principal who said the white girls were exceedingly fond of the colored girls, and she wondered if it ought to be encouraged.

Her query seemed to be based on her feeling as to the social difference between the girls.

Reports on conduct varied widely in the schools, some reporting no trouble at all while others complained of much unruliness. Several reasons were assigned for the trouble. Bad home influence or no home influence were among them, the latter when the parents or guardians were at work and the children were left alone to roam the streets. Bad tone on the streets, soliciting by prostitutes, bad language, and a large amount of lounging on street corners were also thought to be responsible for trouble, because of their effect on the morals of the children.

Two principals, in the first interviews, reported cases of unmarried mothers, and said the conduct in school of the girls in question was so exemplary and their regard for these girls had been so high, they would have trusted them anywhere. Freedom from restraint at home was thought to be largely responsible for this trouble, and the custom of admitting lodgers to the families in which there were young girls was deprecated. The practice of receiving lodgers was said to be prevalent because of the high rents charged colored people, usually two or three dollars a month being added to the rent of each apartment in a house when it was opened to colored tenants.

Several principals felt the need for a parental school for girls, and regretted that certain girls who had been guilty of sex immorality should be in the schools associating with other children. These girls had been found writing obscene notes both to boys and to other girls, and it was generally felt that they had a bad influence on the other children both in the schools and out.

Thieving from both teachers and pupils was complained of. One high school principal said he had formerly believed colored girls were more inclined to be lightfingered than white girls, but that he had come to modify this and now thought the proper generalization to be that all girls seemed less observant of property rights than boys because they had a smaller number of pockets in which to conceal their personal belongings from one another.

The most interesting opinions, and, in the nature of things, the most authoritative, concerned the scholarship of colored pupils as distinguished from the white.

This scholarship was said to be affected by the following conditions:

First: Large numbers of colored children have come to New York from the South, who, at ten or twelve years of age, either had never been in school or whose training had been of such inferior quality that it necessitated practically a fresh start in the lowest grades.

The following letter, received by a colored college president from a colored teacher of the largest county school in one of the southern states, illustrates the quality of the teaching these boys and girls receive. This teacher is paid $14 a month for teaching over 100 children:

"my 12, 19012*

"Prof.——— I drop yo this card to let you know that i will be on that train Munday morning. tell mrs.——— to meet the train.

Yours———"

Second: Scholarship is greatly affected by the instability of the school life of the colored children because of the frequent shifting of occupation and residence of their parents. Colored men and women who go to Florida, the West Indies, Bermuda, etc., for hotel service during the tourist season, take their children out of public school and either take them with them or place them in a boarding school. The children then return to school in the spring, or perhaps not until the fall term of the next year.

These seemed to be the two most important factors in bringing about a low average in the standing of colored pupils.

Third: Another factor bearing on scholarship was the amount of work performed at home by some of the children. As an illustration, a principal cited the case of a boy who seemed hopelessly stupid. It was found that as a rule he was obliged to remain awake until one o'clock in the morning because his grandmother with whom he lived owned a small restaurant and, as she was unable to count, it devolved upon this boy to make change until the restaurant closed.

Fourth: Lack of help with home studies, due to illiteracy or poor education on the part of the parents, was given as an additional handicap to good scholarship as contrasted with American-born white children in the same schools.

It was felt, however, that as a whole the colored children were making normal progress under normal conditions; that is, in cases where they had attended schools in New York City regularly,

* Reprinted from "The Crisis."

their progress was on a par with the white children in the same schools.

Next to the great problem of defective scholarship came truancy, which was causing much trouble in all the schools, the offenders being both boys and girls of all ages. In Public School 89, the only school in which the figures were available for colored pupils, 500 offenders had been reported to the attendance officer during the school year, and between forty and fifty boys were continuously on probation.

The principal in another school in this district said that because of the delay in the reports on truants from attendance officers, much better results had been obtained by either making inquiry herself at the child's home or having her clerk do so. In other schools either the clerk or head of department was following up absences closely and persistently, with excellent results, but it was generally felt that this method was effective only in incipient cases and with the younger children. For the older boys, especially where there was a lack of restraint at home, it was thought that confinement in an institution or parental school afforded the only reliable remedy, and this in spite of the delay in the process of commitment. Often this delay would be so great that arrest for delinquency was more than likely to ensue before such commitment could be arranged.

Principals felt that sending notes to parents did little good in cases of truancy because the parents either did not receive the notes at all, as the pupils themselves abstracted them from the mail-boxes, or, if they did receive the notes, nothing was accomplished as many of them could not read. Several of the principals were accustomed themselves to go out after absentees, often bringing in from the street three or four at one time; but no satisfactory solution of the attendance problem had yet been reached.

In schools where a visiting teacher had been active for a time, the trouble with attendance was found to be mitigated to a marked degree. One of the visiting teachers of the Public Education Association who had a number of colored pupils in her district, said she attributed the tendency to truancy very largely to the lack of compulsory education laws in the south or to the actual lack of school accommodations for colored children in many of the southern states. The children who came here from the south had not had the school habit inculcated in them, and it was difficult to make parents understand that attendance was compulsory in the New York schools. Once such an understanding had been effected and she had established friendly relations with the boys and girls, she had little trouble; but continuous, close-knit work had been necessary in order to secure results.

The school authorities almost unanimously ascribed the large amount of truancy among colored boys and girls to the fact that so many of the colored mothers worked and the children, coming home to solitary lunches, succumbed to the temptation not to return to school after lunch; or, in cases where mothers left home in the early morning before the children were awake, leaving no one to waken and hurry them off to school, they preferred on finding that they were late not to go to school at all.

As with all races and kinds of children, a favorite method of escaping school attendance was said to be the request for a transfer to another city because of removal of the family. This is such a frequent difficulty that it has been proposed that the National Bureau of Education shall be asked to formulate a plan of interurban transfer.

Closely connected with the problems within the schools was that of the future employment of colored boys and girls. In the high schools and trade schools the case of the colored boy and girl differed from that of white pupils mainly because of the difficulty principals and others who were interested found in securing employment for colored pupils. There was little or no knowledge of how colored boys and girls who had graduated or left school and had secured employment for themselves were earning their living, but there was a general belief among school principals, social workers and colored clergymen that the restriction of industrial opportunities because of their race was sapping the ambition of the colored boys and girls, and that they were not making the effort put forth by their parents and grandparents to secure an education.

The future prospects of the colored children, said most of the principals, gave them much food for thought and constituted a serious difficulty in dealing with school problems. For instance, a principal whose experience had included colored, Italian and Jewish children, said he did not find any distinguishing mark of scholarship in any one of these races, but that he could not conscientiously give the colored children the same reasons or incentives for doing good work that he could give to the children of other races. He said, for example, that if a white boy did not achieve accuracy in his arithmetic or neatness in his writing or ciphering, he could warn that boy of a handicap in the event of his becoming a clerk or a bookkeeper; whereas he could not hold out to a colored boy the same prospect of a position either as a clerk or as a bookkeeper.

The principals of the Vocational School for Boys and the Manhattan Trade School also dwelt upon the uncertainty of securing employment for colored pupils. Twenty-five unsuccessful applications for work had been made in behalf of a boy who had qualified as a machine-shop apprentice, and who, to quote the principal, "was the kind of boy I would want my own son to be." The principal said that this difficulty was due to the unwillingness of the unions in the skilled trades to admit colored members, to whom, he said, these unions were to all intents and purposes "closed corporations."

In the Manhattan Trade School, the principal stated that the dressmaking department afforded the best opportunity for colored girls so far as placing them was concerned, but that even in this field she had much trouble. She said that she had found herself obliged to demand a higher standard of qualification for admission to the school from the colored girls than she did from the white girls because of the difficulty she had in persuading employers to accept them. Besides this, she could not accept more than a certain percentage of colored pupils because if the number were to grow into anything like an equal proportion of white and black pupils, she believed that the white girls would not come to the school and it would become a school for colored girls only. This principal said that no effort had been made to learn what avenues of employment there were for colored girls among colored people.

The problem of vocational guidance was causing much perplexity to the high school principals as well. One principal said his own judgment inclined him to advise dentistry, forestry, scientific farming or the ministry as offering the most likely field for colored boys. In the course of this conversation, one of the boys was met in the hallway of the school and the principal asked him what he had in mind as an occupation after he left school. The boy said that his best work had been in mechanical drawing and he hoped to make use of this ability. He thought he might be able to secure work in an architect's office and become a draughtsman. The principal, however, was skeptical of his chance for success in this field.

Almost nothing could be learned about the work being done by pupils who had graduated or left school, because of the lack of first-hand knowledge by teachers and principals of the home conditions of the colored children. The amount of home visiting by teachers was almost negligible owing to the prevailing belief that it would not be right or proper for young women to go into colored homes. Most principals did not encourage home visiting among their colored pupils and several said they would not permit it.

Nevertheless, the school nurses reported uniformly courteous treatment and much appreciation by the colored parents they visited. Two of these nurses said they had occasionally come into homes during the day where they found men and women drinking beer and playing cards together, but that no objectionable language or actions had come to their notice. As all these nurses were young women, it was difficult to understand the distinction existing in the minds of the principals between the probable safety of nurses and of teachers in paying visits. Any inquiry for an explanation of this distinction was invariably met with: "The situation is quite different. The nurses have a good reason for calling, and their profession protects them." They also thought that if only one teacher were to meet with disaster, any probable good to be accomplished by visiting the homes would be more than offset.

The police officers were of the same opinion, and cautioned the investigator against going into colored tenements without leaving a record of her route at the station-house.

It was stated that there was great difficulty in securing the attendance of colored mothers at mothers' meetings held in the afternoon, because most of the colored women were employed during the day. It was suggested that the fact of their being employed might also account for their failure to respond to notes asking them to see the principal or the teacher concerning the discipline of the children. As a matter of fact, later inquiry proved that this was really the case, one mother after another stating that every time she went to the school it cost her from a quarter to a half-day's pay. The supposed danger in visiting the homes of colored school children constituted the greatest objection to meetings for mothers in the evenings, for even if the teachers were willing to give up evenings for that purpose, their families would not permit them to go at night into neighborhoods where colored families lived.

For the most part the principals and teachers were glad of an opportunity to have the homes of the colored children visited with a view to bringing about a better understanding of conditions by both parents and school authorities, and in only three instances was coöperation refused.* When the investigation opened none of the schools in which there were colored pupils were equipped with the helpful social activities that have been inaugurated in other schools. With the exception of branches of the Public Schools Athletic League (which are too impersonal to constitute a really social activity), nothing recreational was provided. During the year, however, walking and swimming clubs were formed in two schools, and an afternoon playground had been opened in a third. These activities were for the white as well as for the colored children.

None of the schools, with the exception of the Henrietta Industrial School, served school luncheons, nor were there in existence any of the Little Mothers' Leagues conducted by the Board of Health in a number of public schools. In two schools Waring Juvenile Leagues had been started, a colored girl being secretary of one of them. At the general session of the leagues, at which the secretaries of the various sections read their reports, the colored girl's report was considered the ablest one read. One of the patronesses of the leagues raised the question as to the desirability of membership for colored children, on the score that one of them might possibly be elected president. This is a good illustration of the present ambiguous mental state of society regarding segregation.

The afternoon playground mentioned above was opened in Public School 89 during the winter of 1912–1913, and has developed mainly along the lines of a practice ground for the various church and settlement basket-ball teams. There was little organized play, the director finding it difficult to interest colored boys in the games ordinarily popular in these centers. About 150 boys attended the playground each afternoon, running in and out continually. There was steadily growing interest in the basket-ball games, however, and the director of the play-

* Vocational School for Boys, Washington Irving High School and Public School 87.

ground felt that if a number of young men could be interested
to give their services at the center, becoming friends with the
boys, individual boys needing attention might thus be reached.

No figures showing the percentage of poor scholarship, attendance, etc., for colored children as a group were available as no
record is kept separately for colored children in any of the schools.

This preliminary inquiry indicated that the needs of colored
pupils in the schools were, roughly:

1. A special arrangement of studies for overage pupils.

2. After-school care for children of working parents.

3. A better understanding between homes and schools brought
about by the visiting teachers, mothers' clubs, etc.

4. School lunches.

5. Prompt and close following up of absences as a preventive
of chronic truancy.

6. A more thorough study of opportunities for employment of
boys and girls.

7. Care by principals that no race feeling is manifested by
teachers or pupils.

These needs and suggestions for meeting them will be dealt
with more fully in the chapter on Needs and Recommendations.

II. Social Agencies

In this preliminary survey of the social agencies of the city,
both public and private, no attempt was made to study the activities of the general agencies or gauge the value of their work.
Opinions were sought from members of the staff of each organization as to the need by colored people for the work done by
the agency in question, and just how much of such work it was
already doing or could do in the future. Any opinion bearing
upon the subject in general was welcomed as throwing light on
the attitude of the organization toward the assistance or improvement of colored children. In the case of those agencies dealing
solely with Negroes, on the other hand, an effort was made to
become acquainted with all the forms of activity they represented
and also the general aim or purpose of each particular agency.
Comment or criticism naturally came to the investigator's mind
as a result of such conferences, and wherever it seemed as if such
comments threw light on the situation they were included. In
describing such a hasty survey over so large a field it is impossible to make a succession of orderly statements. An informal

array of opinion and comment is the only possible method of presenting this material. The aim has been to give as vivid a picture as possible of the variety of sentiment encountered concerning colored people as well as of the efforts being made to meet their many and very evident needs.

In studying the social agencies, the city departments were visited first. Neither the Tenement House Department nor the Board of Health had any information or figures dealing especially with colored school children, except the general impressions of the school nurses in the latter department. Four of the school nurses, whose duties took them into the homes of colored people, said they found the children clean and well fed, as a rule, and self-reliant to a marked degree; but so far as remedying physical defects was concerned, the colored parents required much following up and were fond of applying remedies recommended by the corner druggist. No figures concerning general health or specific defects were available because no separate records were kept for colored children. All the nurses remarked on the large number of colored men they found at home during the daytime, and thought that it indicated a high percentage of unemployment by the men. They were inclined to think that the colored women supported the family in many cases, while the men were idle.

In the Police Department, both in Harlem and in the San Juan Hill district, inspectors and captains said, without mincing their words, that they considered the colored people worthless, and that it was "useless to bother with them." So long as they did not murder each other, the police said, they did not pay any attention to them but "let them do as they pleased." They said it was useless to follow up complaints because of the tendency to withdraw charges as soon as an investigation by the police was undertaken.

Social workers, on the other hand, complained that the police were neglectful of their duties in colored districts. A number of reasons for this were advanced. It was said that at police headquarters a mistaken feeling of pity for colored people, because of general prejudice against them, had caused orders to be given out not to be severe with them. Again it was said that the police were afraid to go into the colored tenements because several years ago, during the race riots on San Juan Hill, a policeman had been thrown from the roof of a tenement in that district and killed.

It was also stated that colored people were so accustomed to receiving scant justice in court-rooms that they were panic stricken when confronted with the possibility of contact with the law. This accounted for their unwillingness to press complaints against one another.

There was general and bitter complaint by the parents of the school children against the police. Street fighting, foul language and all manner of indecencies were said to pass unmolested by police interference; and in the blocks having a bad reputation not once was a patrolman found on duty. Three of the mothers in one block in the San Juan Hill district said they had gone to the police station to complain of disorder on the streets and in the houses where they lived, and had been treated by the police as though they themselves were the offenders.

In the San Juan Hill district the social workers, both white and colored, are closely organized into the West End Workers' Association, and they have agitated the matter of police indifference to street disorder until they have succeeded in having the entire personnel of the patrol force changed. In October, 1913, the new patrolmen were said to be handling the situation in a much more satisfactory manner.

In Harlem, however, there was no organized body of social workers, and while organizations and individuals have been working zealously, there was very general complaint of petty thieving, street soliciting and fighting without much help from the police in checking the trouble.

The father of one of the school children stated that so many of his friends had been robbed of their personal possessions that he had formed the habit of placing his "best clothes" in pawn on Monday morning, leaving them with the pawnbroker until Saturday night! In another home a wooden club was hanging behind the door to the hall entrance of the flat, which was said to be for use in an emergency because the mother was at home alone most of the time.

Through reports received from the parents of school children it was finally possible to secure the conviction of a colored man employed as janitor in a large flat-house who had been having immoral relations with young colored boys. The woman who reported this case said she had taken it up with the landlord time after time, without result. The Society for the Prevention of Cruelty to Children, to which the matter was reported, found the man in question had already served two sentences for like offenses, and he is now in the penitentiary with an additional fifteen years to serve.

Another report received in the course of visiting the parents concerned a group of young men who were said to be active in enticing young girls into immoral resorts. This matter was reported to the Committee of Fourteen, and, at the time the investigation closed, the leader of the group had been indicted through the efforts of the Society for the Prevention of Cruelty to Children on the charge of holding a young girl for immoral purposes. He has since been convicted, and is now in Sing Sing.

A notorious poolroom on 135th Street was also reported to the Committee of Fourteen, and has been closed.

The results obtained by the West End Workers' Association on San Juan Hill have demonstrated the value of organized effort, while the cases cited above indicate that much assistance may be had in learning about conditions from the parents of school children.

The Department of Parks and Playgrounds comes directly in contact with the problem of the colored school child only through its recreation house and grounds on West 60th Street between Tenth and Eleventh Avenues. Here the white boys had formerly protested against the presence of colored boys, the director said, and until 1911 few colored boys had attended the center. In that year a boys' club from St. Cyprian's Parish House began using the grounds of this center and at the time of the investigation a number of colored boys were on the basket-ball, baseball, track teams, etc. The director said there had been no actual trouble lately although the white boys made more or less complaint because of the presence of colored boys.

There are no parks whatever in that section of Harlem in which colored people live, and no out-of-door playground space for the colored children of this district except occasional vacant lots in which itinerant carousels and moving picture shows pitch their tents during the summer. These resorts were badly supervised and there was much complaint from parents of disorder and questionable practices. The police apparently paid little attention to these places, and judging from verbal reports of what took place there, the resorts were not by any means desirable places for growing boys and girls to frequent without supervision. An attempt was made to induce the Board of Estimate and Apportionment to purchase property between 139th and 140th Streets, running from Lenox to Seventh Avenues, for a public playground, but the plan did not succeed.

Few of the recreation centers conducted by the Board of Education are located in the districts in which colored people live. The center in the building of the High School of Commerce, on 64th Street, between Broadway and Amsterdam Avenue, and that in Public School 89, at 134th Street and Lenox Avenue, were the only evening centers in which any colored boys were found. No colored girls were in attendance at either of them.

The center in the High School of Commerce is thoroughly equipped with every possible device for athletic games and exercises, including a swimming pool, shower baths, running track, arena, and apparatus of all kinds. There was an average attendance of about 250 nightly, and perhaps a dozen colored boys were present each of the three times visits were made at this center. The feeling between them and the white boys was evidently friendly and the director said their most popular runner was a colored boy. Several years ago this center was the scene of a race riot which the director said had occurred after a personal encounter between two boys, one white and one colored, who jostled each other while watching an exhibition of track running. The white boy was said to be a $7-a-week messenger of the Interborough Rapid Transit Company, while the colored boy was a college graduate, several years the senior of the white boy, a $1500-a-year employee of the Department of Water Supply, Gas and Electricity, and a member of a club of colored young men who had been meeting in one of the rooms in the center. These club members had not "mixed" with the white boys, who were their inferiors in education and who resented the fancied exclusiveness of the colored boys, so that only the shadow of an excuse was necessary to cause trouble. The director believed that the same trouble would have happened if a club of white boys had adopted the same attitude towards the boys who attended the regular activities of the center, of which clubs do not form a part.

The director also said that an effort had been made by colored social workers to establish clubs for colored boys at the center, but he felt that anything of this nature would precipitate trouble. Any boy who came and made a place for himself as an individual and was willing to be accepted on his merits would have no trouble, but the hard feeling of several years ago was only just being forgotten, and the director felt that no chance should be taken of disturbing the existing friendly relations between the white and colored boys.

Another official of the Board of Education said he would be sorry to have clubs exclusively for colored boys started in the schools, as it might prove the entering wedge that would destroy the anti-segregation policy of the public schools.

In the center at Public School 89 the situation was different in that over 90 per cent. of the boys were colored and it did not seem probable that any difficulty of the nature of that experienced downtown would arise. This playground was, however, not well equipped. It was opened in February, 1912, and aside from basket-ball, had no organized work. A game room was attempted but was not successful. A singing club for adults was successful, however, and had assisted in furnishing the entertainment at several public meetings held in the school house.

The night schools largely attended by colored people, noticeably those in Public School 89 and in Public School 67, 120 West 46th Street, were adding social features in the form of monthly assemblies at which programs were offered by the pupils of the schools. These night schools, however, were attended almost exclusively by adults.

The only afternoon public school playground attended by colored children which was open during the winter was the one at Public School 89. There were, also, two summer playgrounds which were visited, both located in Harlem. They were not satisfactory so far as the colored children were concerned. In one no program was followed and the boys ran in and out in a disorderly manner; the evil effects of this would of course react on all the children, both white and colored. In the kindergarten division, the only one to which girls were admitted, there were, on the four occasions it was visited, only ten or twelve colored children and they were standing about listlessly, no attention being paid to them. In the other playground the situation was better, so far as the games were concerned. In the free play and in the kindergarten work, however, no attention whatever was paid to the colored children by the workers. The director said it was difficult to interest them, but in the games witnessed they were alert and often successful. Both these playgrounds contrasted unfavorably with the summer playgrounds at Stillman House and at the New York Free Kindergarten Association for Colored Children which were successfully conducted, the children remaining all day, leaving the premises only at noon.

In the Department of Charities, in the minds of the authorities no problem regarding colored people seemed to exist. It was said that no distinctions were made, and no separate records were kept.

The Children's Court, however, presented one of the most acute problems encountered during the entire period of the investigation. At the time the investigation was undertaken, December 15, 1912, there were no means of caring for delinquent colored girls under sixteen years of age in institutions. A letter written by Mr. Thomas D. Walsh, Superintendent of the Society for the Prevention of Cruelty to Children, to the National League on Urban Conditions Among Negroes, stated that "it would be futile to take the case of a young colored girl into the Children's Court, as at this time there is no provision for their care in any institution . . ." This meant that the State Training School for delinquent girls under sixteen years of age, at Hudson, New York, was quarantined because of an epidemic of trachoma, and that Catholic and Protestant private institutions admitted only two or three colored girls each.

These girls were therefore being referred informally to the National League on Urban Conditions Among Negroes by the Society for the Prevention of Cruelty to Children, and the League was attempting to cope with the situation by means of an as yet unorganized corps of colored Big Sisters, and an endeavor to coöperate in raising $5000 a year for three years to start a home for young delinquent colored girls. The necessary result was that the girls were merely being sent back to their homes, where it was difficult if not impossible to prevent them from going into the streets again. In some cases they went back to the school rooms, although some of them, twelve and fourteen years old, were mothers.

Judge Franklin C. Hoyt, of the Children's Court, said the situation was most acute; that it was the more dangerous because the colored girls themselves were fully alive to it, and the spirit of bravado among them was rendering it increasingly difficult for him to do anything with them.

In sending the delinquent colored girls back to their homes, the Society for the Prevention of Cruelty to Children departed from its usual custom of holding juvenile delinquents in its detention home until there was institutional accommodation for them.

On account of the unorganized state of the "Colored Big Sisters" referred to above, it was difficult, if not impossible for the officers of the League to know whether the friendly visitors whom they had appointed had reached the girls or not. The head of the Catholic mission work for colored people in New York City was consulted as to the reason why Catholic institutions were refusing to admit colored girls. He said he had no knowledge of their refusal to do so and would take up the matter at once. Soon after this the House of the Good Shepherd accepted colored girls as inmates, and a new wing to the institution has since been built to accommodate them.

No definite response was received from similar Protestant institutions when the question was raised as to their attitude in this question.

When the quarantine at the State Training School for girls at Hudson, New York, was lifted, Dr. Hortense V. Bruce, the superintendent, was visited and asked for her opinion on the general situation as it related to delinquent colored girls.

Miss Bruce said she felt the colored girl presented a special problem which complicated the already sufficiently difficult one at Hudson, of attempting to reform 365 delinquent girls under sixteen years of age. She said the colored girls who came to her differed from the majority of the white girls in the training school in that they had none of the vicious habits and practices of the white girls. There was a difference of opinion on this point, however, among other officers of the Training School. The difference in color, Miss Bruce said, appealed to the white girls in much the same way as a difference in sex, and the association of the two races led to abnormal practices. She said, too, that the colored girls' sense of humor upset the discipline of the classes they attended and that the house mothers found them more difficult to train and control than were the white girls. How far the house mothers were influenced by their objection to colored girls *per se* Miss Bruce was unwilling to say; but she acknowledged that she had great difficulty in finding house mothers for the two cottages (housing twenty-four girls each) to which colored girls were assigned, and in keeping them contented and happy after she had found them.

The whole problem of young delinquent colored girls could be handled much more satisfactorily in a separate institution, Miss Bruce thought, if such an institution could be officered properly. She was inclined to favor separate buildings, with a corps of colored workers, on another portion of the state grounds and under her own superintendence. She felt that any extensive enlargement of the Training School would decrease the efficiency of the work done there; but, on the other hand, felt that the delinquent girl was a problem for the state and not for private philanthropy to deal with.

Miss Bruce said the placing in situations of girls who leave the Training School was a difficult problem, as the opportunity for colored girls to secure employment was limited to an unusual degree at best. She said she would welcome coöperation with some organized activity in New York to help in dealing with this problem.

There are no separate cottages for the colored girls at Bedford Reformatory, but each girl is placed where her merits of conduct and work entitle her to go according to the discipline of the institution. Miss Katherine B. Davis, at that time superintendent of Bedford, felt that nothing would be gained by separating the girls in cottages, as they slept in separate rooms, and whether one roof or several covered these rooms made no difference. In institutions where the girls slept in dormitories she thought a night guard would solve the problem of any improper conduct.

It had been suggested to the Bedford Board of Managers at one time that the colored girls should be segregated because it was a social misdemeanor for white girls to associate with them in normal society and therefore this association should not be permitted in a reformatory. The Board of Managers had not, however, seen its way to comply with this request because they felt such a procedure would interfere with the dispensing of equal justice to everyone in the reformatory.

It was also stated that the colored girls were the best probationers and that it was far easier to secure employment for them because of their willingness to enter domestic service, where they were able to accumulate substantially more savings than were the white girls who went into shops and factories. Although many of the probationers lapsed into sex errors from time to time, the colored girl was apparently far less liable than the white girl to adopt prostitution as a means of livelihood.

Miss Davis was asked for her opinion as to the advisability of increasing the number of private institutions for delinquent boys and girls. She said she was unqualifiedly opposed to private institutions and thought that every effort should be bent on forcing the state to provide adequately for delinquents. She said the new detention house, now nearing completion in New York City, ought to put an end to the necessity for turning back into the schools or onto the streets those boys and girls who had been convicted of misdemeanors and for whom there was no accommodation in state institutions; and that philanthropic agencies would perform an infinitely greater service by providing means for training boys and girls to earn a livelihood than by attempting to continue what was in her opinion a duty that should be delegated to the state.

In discussing the general character of the colored girl offender, the Judge of the Children's Court said that he, too, found her a different type from the white girl; that while she seemed to fall into sex errors more readily than did the white girl, yet such a lapse did not make her vicious nor did it cause a breakdown of her whole nature, as it was apt to do with girls of other races. He ascribed this largely to the fact that the colored girls' families did not discard them, and that almost without exception the colored girls cared for and supported their illegitimate children, as a matter of course.

In the fall of 1913 the situation as it concerned the delinquent colored girl was much relieved by the opening of the House of the Good Shepherd to colored girls; and after September, 1913, there was no necessity of sending any girl requiring institutional care to her home because of lack of accommodation in an institution. The situation as it exists today * presents the difficulty of caring for Protestant colored girls in a Catholic institution; if the Protestant institutions were to follow the example of the House of the Good Shepherd and admit colored girls, and if additional accommodations were secured for them at the Hudson Training School, the situation would be more adequately met.

The Secretary of the New York Probation Society, when consulted concerning the rehabilitation of delinquent colored girls, said that the colored people seem always to have shown the char-

* August, 1914.

ity toward young offenders and the sense of responsibility of unmarried mothers for their children that our newest conception of morality is teaching white people. When colored girls were cast off by their families, however, or when they had no families, they went to pieces more completely than did the white girls with whom the society had had experience, for not content with becoming prostitutes they were the most dangerous "badgers" she had known.

The Superintendent of the Society for the Prevention of Cruelty to Children said he had not much hope of rehabilitating colored girls of the type his society took into custody. He said they had no conception of morals and were so untruthful that he found it difficult to secure adequate testimony on which to convict men accused of harming them, even when he had corroborating testimony. He thought more work should be done to raise the morals of the race.

There was apparently little trouble in placing delinquent colored boys, as the House of Refuge on Randall's Island could always be depended upon in any ordinary circumstances.

Petty thieving appeared to be the most frequent charge against the boys; but grand larceny and more serious misdemeanors were said to be increasing, especially in the Harlem district.

It was not possible to secure the percentages of kinds of offenses for which either boys or girls were sent to institutions, as the records for colored cases were not kept separately.

Neither the Children's Court nor the Society for the Prevention of Cruelty to Children had a colored probation officer or investigator on its staff. The Children's Court, however, makes a definite effort to have equal time and attention given to colored and white children, and the Superintendent of the Society for the Prevention of Cruelty to Children said he was ready to consider employing a colored investigator. He received much valuable assistance, he said, from the National League on Urban Conditions Among Negroes in investigating his cases of colored children.

The work of the Big Brothers and Big Sisters is so intimately connected with the delinquent child who comes before the Children's Court that although they are private philanthropic bodies, they have a semi-official standing in the Court. Certain of the milder forms of delinquency and of improper guardianship are assigned to them for the peculiar service rendered by their respective organizations: i. e., attempting to influence the lives of these boys and girls by means of a friendship with persons of presumably strong character who possess the qualifications fitting them for this work of voluntary social service.

Aside from the consultation in court and referring the children to agencies who in turn attempt to secure friendly visitors for them, neither the Big Brothers nor the Big Sisters parent organizations extend their work to the colored people. The National League on Urban Conditions Among Negroes is striving to organize Big Brothers and Big Sisters among the colored people; but these colored workers are not admitted to membership in the parent organizations, no reports of their work go to the parent bodies, and nothing is known in the central offices of the results obtained.

One of the volunteer Big Sisters in the Children's Court complained that the colored women were not responding with any degree of enthusiasm to the appeal for help that had been made by the Big Sisters in behalf of the colored girls who were appearing before the Children's Court. When the question was raised as to admitting colored women to membership in the parent organization, since if they were intelligent enough and had sufficiently high standards to be Big Sisters it was a bit difficult to understand why they should be barred from such membership, the reply by a member of the Board of Managers of the Big Sisters society was that this was impossible because it seemed to imply a sort of equality which it was unwise to foster.

Inability to become a member of the parent organization bars a colored Big Brother or Big Sister from the very real benefit of attending the meetings and hearing reports and discussions and being in touch at first hand with the work done by others with a wider experience than they themselves may have. Whether this deprivation may be offset in some way is a question to be answered. Consciousness of this difference undoubtedly affects the enthusiasm, as its results limit the efficiency of the colored worker.

Little that was pertinent to colored children could be learned at the hospitals and dispensaries. Beyond a tendency to rickets, which the colored children were said to share with the Italians, they appeared to present no special problem. At the Harlem Hospital it was said that young colored girls coming for treatment for venereal diseases had been found by the visiting nurse to have given assumed names and addresses, and their cases could therefore neither be registered with the Board of Health nor could their parents be consulted.

In the libraries it was said that there was an increasing after-school attendance by colored children. The librarians have taken much interest, apparently, in the home life of the children and gave substantially the same information as the schools concerning conditions. In the Carnegie Library on West 135th Street, the reading room was used by a number of colored men who worked at night and who, the librarian said, had no other place in which to spend their leisure time unless they went to moving picture shows, pool rooms or political clubs. There was no club house for colored men in this part of the city, but the colored branch of the Young Men's Christian Association was soon to move up from West 53rd Street and this need would then be met.

GENERAL PRIVATE AGENCIES

Aside from the work of the city departments and of the quasi-public institutions—hospitals, libraries, etc.—the situation as it concerns the social agencies of the city and their relation to the colored population is a complicated one. Private philanthropic agencies dealing with special problems, *i. e.*, the relief agencies, Children's Aid Society, Society for the Prevention of Cruelty to Children, etc., differentiate their work for colored people to a greater or less degree; and in some instances, as, for example, in the case of the Big Brothers, Big Sisters, the fresh-air homes of the Association for Improving the Condition of the Poor, etc., colored people are omitted altogether from the activities of the parent bodies although these coöperate to some extent with colored agencies dealing with the same problem.

This differentiation, which might not in itself be objectionable, creates a difficult situation because the large agencies soliciting funds for dealing with a given problem do not contribute from those funds to the agencies dealing exclusively with the colored portion of the problem. These are, therefore, almost without exception, handicapped in their efforts by lack of funds and of trained workers. Colored workers have no opportunity to secure practical experience with agencies whose methods are accepted as standard and it has therefore devolved upon volunteer boards of directors of activities for colored people to train their own workers. It would be obviously unfair, under such conditions, to apply the same standards to work performed or to the results obtained.

There is a difference of opinion as to whether white or colored workers can best carry on the work of social education among the colored people. While naturally sympathy and understanding for the unfortunate of their race are more likely to be found among the colored workers, it is urged that academic training afforded by universities and schools of philanthropy has thus far been the only kind available for colored workers. They have had no opportunity for day-by-day training under expert scrutiny and criticism, thus gaining an experience upon which alone sound judgment in dealing with individual problems may be based. The majority of colored workers have been trained as teachers and their work, as a rule, bears the stamp of the classroom. Only a few have a sufficiently wide vision to overcome this. In consequence, the child attending settlement clubs and classes with colored leaders merely transfers himself from one classroom atmosphere to another and his need for social development is not met.

The director of the Russell Sage Foundation's Department of Surveys and Exhibits stated as his impression from surveys in southern cities that it was difficult to secure good results from activities for colored people carried on by colored workers because so many were not properly equipped educationally and not trained by standard methods. If colored workers could be found who possessed the qualifications demanded by recognized standards, he felt that their employment should by all means follow; if not, then white workers should be employed.

If social work for colored people must be differentiated by social agencies, the question arises whether it may not be both just and expedient for such agencies to create their own departments for this work and train their workers, whether white or colored, by the same methods.

The failure of the majority of the large agencies to apply their program to white and colored alike, leading as it has to the creation of separate agencies for colored people, has made difficult the application of what have come to be regarded as the best methods of dealing with the problems of school children. This is especially true of the work of the visiting teacher, perhaps the most vital force at present available for dealing with those problems. The value of the visiting teacher depends so entirely on the training, judgment, personality and the right mixture of tact and authority of the worker that here, perhaps more than anywhere else, is required standardization of method, continuity and concentration of effort, and the intelligent criticism made possible by assembling all the workers in this field under the auspices of one organization whose work has been stamped as successful. Because of the separation of the social agencies for colored people from the corresponding general agencies there has been created a situation which renders it difficult for those organizations that are prepared to apply their programs to both white and colored people to proceed without conflicting in some degree with the colored workers; and throughout the study, as well as in making recommendations, this situation had to be kept constantly in mind.

Illustrations of follow-up work on the part of various social agencies to which cases reported from the schools were referred show that unless the parents themselves were capable of coping with the situation, either nothing at all was accomplished or the child was committed to institutional care. It was not possible to give to each of the special cases the amount of attention it required,—the kind of attention given to this type of child by the visiting teacher,—and those cases referred to settlements, Boy Scouts, etc., while placed in touch with the programs of the various organizations, were either not watched with sufficient care or were in the first place not given the proper sort of treatment their especial difficulty required. Examples of such cases are found in Appendix I.

On the other hand, in spite of the fact that some of the most difficult children referred by the principals had been for years members of the clubs and classes in the various social centers, the workers in these clubs not only were unaware of any trouble in school but had not discovered that the child had any special need, whether spiritual or material.

A worker in one of the centers spoke of the difficulty she was having with a boy whose mother worked every day and had asked her to care for him after school. The boy often failed to make his appearance and the worker in question said she had never been able to win him over so that she felt she could rely on him. In discussing the case it transpired that the boy had threatened on several occasions to commit suicide. When asked if she had ever secured his school record or had him examined for feeblemindedness or insanity, she said it had never occurred to her to do either.

Many of the general private agencies were interviewed and information sought as to the application of their work to colored children. One of the Secretaries of the State Charities Aid Association said their work touched colored children only in the child-placing department and that they did not care to go very deeply into the matter of placing colored children. They placed them when necessary, but were not making the work a part of their program. She said they had difficulty in finding desirable homes. This matter was taken up later with the secretary in charge of the work with girls for the National League on Urban Conditions Among Negroes who said that few of the white agencies knew the better class of colored people. Co-operation was suggested with the National League on Urban Conditions Among Negroes with a view to finding through them a better grade of home for the State Charities Aid Association's colored children. The suggestion was favorably received and the Association's child-placing agent got in touch with the League and found desirable boarding places for children through them, but no homes into which the children were taken without pay.

The Probation Society reported that it was overwhelmed with work; the Secretary felt that the problem of the colored girl was a distinct one and should be taken care of by those interested in it. When asked if an arrangement would not be possible whereby the Probation Society might employ a worker for colored cases, such a worker, however, to be responsible to the Secretary so that the whole probation problem would be in the hands of one organization, she said that such an arrangement would undoubtedly be the more logical one, but at present the burden on the Society was so great that it would not be possible to undertake further work.

The Director of the Prison Association said his Association had its hands so full of work that they had no opportunity even to think of the problems of the colored people, which he said he realized required special consideration because of the variety of community sentiment concerning Negroes.

Neither the Woman's Municipal League nor the Women's Health Protective Association admitted colored members, and neither organization had thus far concerned itself with districts in which colored people lived.

The Association for Improving the Condition of the Poor, with the largest equipment for carrying on fresh-air work of perhaps any organization in the world, limited its work with colored people to two day parties for colored mothers and babies to Sea Breeze. Those of its relief cases requiring a change of air were sent to a small summer camp maintained by one of the day nurseries for colored children. Some one interested in the investigation visited this place and found it quite primitive and devoid of all the educational features of the Association's institutions. All the guests, however, appeared to be enjoying themselves and were in good health.

The Tribune Fresh Air Fund was sending its colored beneficiaries to a farm maintained by a colored ex-clergyman on Long Island. Colored social workers said the management of this farm was not up to the standard demanded and obtained elsewhere by the Colored Fresh Air Committee, this Committee being made up of representative social workers, white as well as colored.

This state of affairs concerning the fresh-air work of the large agencies led to an inquiry of the Bureau of Advice and Information of the Charity Organization Society, for a report on the entire fresh-air situation as it had to do with colored children. They wrote as follows:

"JULY, 1913.

"Fresh-air work for colored children in New York is very inadequately co-ordinated and so little data is accessible that a special investigation would be necessary as a basis for proper organization. Such an investigation was attempted in 1910, when a Central Bureau of Colored Fresh-Air Agencies was established for the purpose of unifying the various activities in this field. This investigation, however, was not successful, lack of money making it impossible to secure expert agents, and the Bureau was discontinued (April, 1911). Its task was handed over to the Committee on Urban Conditions Among Negroes. This Committee had agreed to take over the work on condition that the agencies would co-operate by sending records and using the committee as a clearing house; but this the majority of the agencies failed to do.

"Partly to encourage co-operation, the Committee started a boys' camp, to which all agencies were given the opportunity to send boys for a period of two weeks. The camp was a successful venture and has been continued.

"In the summer of 1912, experiencing the same difficulty in securing records and proper co-operation, the National League on

Urban Conditions Among Negroes proposed that what it regarded as the strongest agency doing fresh-air work for colored children should take over the work entirely, federating with the League if it wished. In this case the League would turn over its camp and equipment, helping further in every way to put the whole service on an efficient basis. The agency chosen, however, felt that it could not undertake that responsibility, and the League on Urban Conditions may be driven to taking over the whole work itself.

"In the event of the League's assuming the responsibility for the fresh-air work among colored children, its budget would need to be extended to cover the salary of an office clerk and two field workers during the summer season. The fresh-air work of the League for the summer of 1912 consisted in placing 591 mothers and babies in fresh-air homes. One hundred and forty-two boys were accommodated for vacations of two weeks at the boys' camp at Verona, New Jersey. This camp is equipped with tents and the sanitary conditions are said to be good. The camp can receive forty boys at a time.

"After the National League on Urban Conditions Among Negroes, the Negro Fresh Air Committee is the leading agency. The chairman of this committee is Rev. William N. Hubbell of St. David's Church in the Bronx. Its leading spirit is Miss Helena Titus Emerson, of the Free Kindergarten Association for Colored Children, 202 West 63rd Street, who has been active in every effort to better conditions in this field. During the summer of 1912 this committee sent 281 families and 833 individuals to the Sea Breeze day excursions of the Association for Improving the Condition of the Poor; 105 persons (including boys, girls and adults) to St. David's Home, the summer home maintained by the City Missions Association at White Plains, New York; 59 boys to the camp of the National League on Urban Conditions Among Negroes at Verona, New Jersey, the fares being paid by the Tribune Fresh Air Fund, board paid by the Negro Fresh Air Committee. Nineteen boys and girls with three nurses were sent to Hawthorne, New York.

"One hundred and sixty children were obliged to remain at home because of lack of funds, accommodations, etc., and 85 mothers and babies were prevented from going to St. David's for the same reason.

"In addition to maintaining this fresh-air work, the committee is making an effort to raise funds for a fresh-air and convalescent home for colored people to be open the year round. There is evidently need for such an institution, as none exists at present."

Valuable fresh-air work has also been done by the New York Colored Mission.

The relief agencies—the Charity Organization Society and the Association for Improving the Condition of the Poor—said their problem of family rehabilitation was complicated in cases of colored people mainly by two conditions: the frequency with which colored men deserted their families, and the neglect of their children by working mothers or other relatives in whose care they were living. Both organizations felt that commitments for improper guardianship and for neglect should be more actively pressed. The Society for the Prevention of Cruelty to Children stated, however, that there would be need for at least two more institutions than are at present in existence, if they were to press all the cases of children who should rightfully be committed for improper guardianship or for neglect.

Attendance officers of the schools, in their turn, criticized the relief agencies and said they personally secured much more prompt and effective help from corner saloons when food and clothing were needed for the families they visited.

Social workers among the colored people stated that the relief agencies were inclined to hold the Negroes to impossible standards, in view of their history and training; and that relief was given much more effectively by the small churches for colored people, where a printed notice to the effect that "Sister———— was in need," brought donations of·bread, flour, etc., to meet the emergency.

Workers in Stillman House, a branch of the Henry Street Settlement, on West 60th Street, devoted to work with colored people, have been much impressed with the self-respecting character of the colored people, as evidenced by the lack of any tendency on their part to beg.

Miss Helena Titus Emerson, a pioneer white worker among colored people, in charge of the social activities of the New York Free Kindergarten Association for Colored Children, also said that once actual need was past, rehabilitation was almost automatic among colored people. Miss Emerson said poverty came most often because of the lack of opportunity to work. The married women or widows with children to support, going out to work by the day as laundresses or house cleaners in white families, were out of work during the summer months when their employers were out of town, and much hardship resulted.

There was little coöperation between the large relief agencies and the societies, organizations, lodges, etc., whose name is legion, giving relief and sick benefits to colored people. On San Juan Hill the colored social workers were on the district committee of the Charity Organization Society, but in Harlem there had been no coöperation between colored and white workers, except in individual cases, until the winter of 1913, when a number of colored workers were called together to form a class in the study of giving relief under the direction of the Charity Organization Society's agent in that district. It was planned first to have a separate advisory committee for the colored people in Harlem, and the Charity Organization Society's agent was given the names of a number of the representative social workers, clergymen, etc., in that district; later, instead of an advisory committee, these workers were formed into a class.

AGENCIES SOLELY FOR COLORED PEOPLE

A. National

Since the Lincoln Centennial—at which time a number of the closest students of the colored problem stated, in an appeal sent to the publicists of the country, "that some ten millions of descendants of former slaves were losing ground almost daily because everywhere they were prevented from securing any but menial work to do; were driven out of anything like desirable living quarters in all large cities; and were in addition subjected to every manner of abuse with no means of redress;"—the growth of social effort by the colored people themselves, as well as by white people in their behalf, has been rapid. Two significant movements having headquarters in New York have been organized, both of national scope and both dealing exclusively with problems of the colored race. The first to enter the field, The National Association for the Advancement of Colored People, concerns itself with the civil status of Negroes and seeks to alleviate the handicap its members believe race discrimination imposes alike on those Negroes who have made themselves efficient and on the most undeveloped members of the race. Concerning its purpose, W. E. B. DuBois, director of publicity and research for the Association, says:

"The National Association for the Advancement of Colored People is working to make practical in New York City and in the nation, a democracy which will not hesitate on the color line; and we believe the discrimination which is called *the Negro problem* is at the bottom of many economic and social troubles which affect not only the colored people, but all Americans. So far as New York City is concerned, the race prejudice against colored people takes especially the form of industrial exclusion, difficulty in finding decent homes, and lack of facility for amusements. These specific difficulties may be ameliorated by various movements; but as long as any large group of people is so despised by their fellows that they can be treated with public contempt, the result will be discrimination of various kinds and lack of opportunity. It is against this fundamental problem of race prejudice that the Association is working."

The Association for the Advancement of Colored People has on its Executive Board representatives of both the white and black races, and numbers among its members Moorfield Storey of Boston, who is the national president; Dr. Joel E. Spingarn, Oswald Garrison Villard, Treasurer, W. E. B. DuBois, William English Walling, Jane Addams, Florence Kelley, Lillian D. Wald, and a number of colored clergymen and social workers.

In New York it is confining its efforts to cases of civil discrimination, and has successfully defended the rights of colored people to occupy seats in any part of a theatre, to be served in restaurants, etc. It is opposed to any form of segregation, believing that separation of the races invariably leads to discrimination against the colored people, giving them inferior schools where separate schools are maintained, inferior cars and accommodations where the so-called "Jim Crow" laws exist, and so through every phase of life.

The Advancement Association has withdrawn from the purely social field in New York City, which it has left to the National League on Urban Conditions Among Negroes. As its name implies, this organization concerns itself with the problems of Negroes which arise through the conditions of their lives in cities. The Board of Directors and membership of the League are made up of both white and colored, in the belief "that the different problems engendered by the close contact of the two races in cities, must have, if they are to be solved, the careful study and sympathetic handling of intelligent and liberal-minded persons of both races." (Statement by directors.)

The League is the outgrowth of three previously existing organizations which found themselves in frequent coöperation. By way of experiment, they came together in 1911 in a loose federation, and then formed in 1912 a closer union under the present name.

The New York program of the League includes a housing bureau to aid in the enforcement of the tenement house law; an employment bureau, not only for securing work for colored people, but also to make a study of the trend of occupations available for them; the organization of Big Brothers and Big Sisters; travellers' aid service; a fresh-air camp for boys; and the organization of agencies to provide probationary and institutional care for delinquent girls and women. In addition to these features the League has promoted conferences among colored social workers, organizations among employed colored men (such as public porters, janitors, etc.), and has striven to aid in the establishment and standardization of social activities in the existing social centers.

Part of the work of the League, as one of the Directors states it, "is to teach the Negro how to use the general agencies for civic betterment rightly, whether public or private. Another part is to induce those agencies not to neglect the Negro, but to realize that, altho Negroes comprise but a small percentage of our total population, they are furnishing a very large proportion of some classes of our civic problems. We initiate no work which is being adequately done by other organizations."

The work of the League is directed by George Edmund Haynes, who has his Ph. D. degree in Sociology from Columbia University and is now Professor of Social Science at Fisk University; and by Eugene Kinckle Jones, who was graduated from Virginia Union University and holds his Master's degree from Cornell. The men who help in the various bureaus have been college students or graduates at Columbia University. Two fellowships have been established by the League. These fellows assist in the work of the various bureaus, and each bureau is supervised by the best people who could be secured as the result of careful search and trial.

Mr. Jones, the associate director, felt that the most acute problems of colored children in New York City were those created by the lack of public recreational facilities; and later on by the restriction in the means of earning their livelihood. He felt that everywhere in the established public playgrounds colored children were discriminated against, while, on the other hand, their homes offered no facilities for recreation. The League was making every effort, Mr. Jones said, to encourage the formation of boys' and girls' clubs where healthy amusement might be available for them. The League had also contemplated undertaking work in vocational guidance for school boys and girls and was about to make an inquiry into occupations already available for them.

The associate director considered also that the bachelor apartments maintained in flats on the west side and in Harlem, which sometimes masqueraded under the name of social clubs and to which girls were brought under various pretenses, constituted a serious menace to the girls who attended the dances and "socials" given in them.

The League has been greatly handicapped by lack of money and the small number of experienced workers from which it can draw. In any criticism of its work these facts must be constantly kept in mind.

The point at which the work of the League touched the investigation most closely was in its school visiting and its work with delinquent boys and girls, and a connection was at once established with these departments which was maintained throughout the investigation. The housing and employment bureaus of the League were also resorted to in a number of instances. Cooperation was sought in various cases of difficult school children reported by school principals. To give instances of cases referred by the investigator to the visitors from the Urban League:

L. Q., a boy, 7 years of age, was reported for irregular attendance. His attendance record was 69%. L. was an exceptionally attractive, likeable child. He was found to be living with his mother's brother and his wife, in a well furnished, comfortable home. It was said that the boy's father was in an insane asylum in the British West Indies and that his mother was living a dissolute life, abandoning the child every few months. The relatives with whom he was living were devoted to the boy and wished to have legal custody of him. Since this seemed to be an instance in which continuous supervision would be desirable the case was referred to the Urban League, first to secure the mother's consent to the boy's adoption, and secondly for preventive care and following up of the future life of the boy. After six weeks, although their worker had gone several times to the address given, she had not found the mother, nor did she know where the boy was, his relatives with whom he lived having moved.

The boy was found in school, his address was learned and also the fact that his mother had been severely burned and was in a hospital, and the case was again referred to the Urban League, but after two months no action had been taken and the boy was being passed from one relative to another. The mother was then seen and she pleaded to be allowed to retain custody of the boy, promising to provide for him any permanent home with relatives that might be approved of.

In the case of S. and M. R., girls, 9 and 10 years old, serious consequences ensued. These two children were reported not only for irregular attendance, but the record of M. showed malnutrition. Their mother had been deserted prior to the birth of a child which was then two months old, and the Charity Organization Society had aided her until her baby was a month old. She then went to live in a boarding house maintained by a small colored mission, where she was visited. She and the two girls scrubbed, cleaned and cooked, and paid in addition $2.00 a week out of the $2.50 Mrs. R. was able to earn washing dishes at night, when she felt she could best leave her baby. The two girls were ragged and unkempt in spite of the fact that the mission house in which they lived maintained sewing classes for children and the woman in charge showed me a number of garments they had made for children. The case was reported to the Urban League, which in turn reported it to an organization of colored women whose president was a member of the Executive Board of the Urban League, and whose club work consisted chiefly in giving relief.

The R. family was visited and the children were given clothing, and employment for the mother was secured.

A month later the family was found by the investigator living in a basement, the girls being kept out of school alternately to care for the baby. A place at the Hope Day Nursery was secured for the baby and the family was again referred to the League. Some weeks later the investigator met the eldest child on Lenox Avenue and asked after the family. She said that the baby was dead, her sister was in St. Joseph's Hospital with tuberculosis, and that she and her mother were still living in the basement. She said that no one from any agency was visiting them. The Urban League's visitor stated that the mother had failed to take advantage of the place secured in the Nursery, that she considered the woman to be slovenly and neglectful of her children, and the case was apparently dropped there.

Another case was that of F. and W. M., two boys 11 and 9 years old respectively. The elder boy had been reported to the Urban League's school visitor at the time this investigation commenced and was later reported to the investigator for the Public Education Association, as no action had apparently been taken. These boys were living on the top floor of a tenement building in the custody of an aunt and a grandmother, both of whom went out to work every day. Their father, a cook in a downtown restaurant, lived elsewhere and although he paid for the boys' maintenance, visited them only once a month.

About two months before the investigation closed the eldest boy was referred as a rapidly retrogressing case. The worker to whom the boys had previously been referred knew nothing of the case but said he would take the boys in hand. He then included W. in a group of boys he was "Big Brothering" and thought W. showed marked improvement after several weeks. In the meantime W. was tested by the Public Education Association field worker, who found him very backward. His brother F., a pathetic little ragged figure with a hoarse cough and dark circles under his eyes, gave no one any trouble and consequently was not even "Big Brothered," but left entirely to his own devices. W., however, steadily improved and seemed to be a credit to his "Big Brother," whose work won the principal's comme ndation.

These were three out of eighteen cases referred to the Urban League. Satisfactory coöperation was not secured in most of them and the follow-up work was seldom thorough.*

Efforts to secure work for individuals through the League's employment bureau were unfortunately not successful, and both the Manhattan Trade School and individual employers said they had not secured results, either in the form of employment or employees, from this bureau.

Coöperation with the housing bureau proved very helpful. Janitor service improved in at least three of the houses reported on the score of poor heat and dilatory collection of garbage, and the bureau reported two houses repaired in which stairs had been found in a dangerous condition. This was brought about by efforts of the League with the landlord, instead of by being reported to the Tenement House Department.

As one of the Directors of the League stated, "the housing bureau is not designed merely to aid in enforcing the tenement house law. It exists for the purpose of studying housing conditions, rents, etc., in Harlem, of teaching the colored people their rights and duties as tenants, and of endeavoring to increase the feeling of responsibility of the landlords and agents to their tenants in the matters of sanitation, repairs, respectability of tenants, etc., and also of raising the standard of janitor service."

The League has also rendeied a most valuable service to the colored community through its promotion of discussions in the churches on city problems: housing reforms, clean streets, etc.

---

* It is probable that the lack of satisfactory work and coöperation in the visits to the cases of difficult school children came about first through a misunderstanding as to the reasons for reporting these cases and then through the fact that the League's visitors were either overworked or untrained. The more such visiting is done the more apparent become two facts—that the full time of a visitor is required and that she must be fitted by training and by experience for her difficult and delicate task.—Editor.

Many leaders among their own people are unalterably opposed to anything that approaches in any particular to a policy of segregation and believe that the best possibility for the development of the Negro race lies in broadening the colored man's contact with white civilization. Many white people believe this. The policy of the League on Urban Conditions seems to be for creating separate agencies for colored people and for employing colored social workers even where their training is not equal to that of available white workers. In that way it appears to the investigator to be encouraging a separation of the efforts for betterment, both personal and civic, of white and colored people, and so failing to stand for the best possible development of the work for colored people in New York City.

The Board of Directors of the League, though composed of persons holding varying opinions on the final status of the Negro, is unanimous in feeling that the Negro needs intelligent help in adjusting himself to city conditions of life and of work. It is at one "in the effort to make of the League an organization to which he will feel free to turn for counsel and encouragement in attacking his own problems. It is a part of the plan that he should recognize in the workers people of his own race who have had to face similar problems of unjust discrimination in many directions—who understand his psychology and his needs as, in the last analysis, only the very exceptional and perhaps no white person can."

The League states that it "aims to co-operate with all and does co-operate with nearly all organizations doing Negro work. . . . Advice is freely offered when asked and the use of the office staff when possible, as for example to the Music School Settlement for which we sent out notices of its first public concert in 1912, to the Negro Fresh Air Committee, which files its statistical records in our office, and to the A. I. C. P. in the matter of its day excursions for Negroes, which latter having been discontinued were finally reëstablished at our instance."

The League naturally has not the support of all the Negroes in New York, but the directors state that as the work and its meaning and spirit are more fully understood, they feel they will rapidly get "the support and sympathy and cordial coöperation of the Negroes, the organizations for Negroes and the general philanthropic agencies, public and private, of the city."

B. New York City

The agencies solely for colored people in New York city have been grouped under the districts in which the schools studied were located. Activities in districts other than these were not visited.

The first district considered, that on San Juan Hill, was more carefully organized than either of the others. The tendency among activities for the betterment of colored people in this district was toward working out a program that would take care of both the economic and cultural development of the neighborhood families. The directory of the various centers in this as well as other colored neighborhoods appended to this report shows in the San Juan Hill neighborhood a Children's Aid Society School; two institutional mission churches; a day nursery; two kindergartens; Stillman House, a settlement to which seven visiting nurses are attached; and a clergyman of the Moravian Church who lives in the model tenements and holds services in the Children's Aid Society School building, all within a radius of three blocks.

One of the most important pieces of work in the San Juan Hill district, from the standpoint of numbers reached, is that done by the Children's Aid Society through its Henrietta Industrial School at 224 West 63rd Street. This school had on its register 465 pupils, with an average daily attendance of 409. It paralleled the work of the public schools through grades 1A to 4B, and in addition conducted classes after school in cobblery, carpentry, sewing, cooking, millinery and chair-caning. Social work and classes were also conducted there in the evening, the families of the children were visited by the teachers, all of whom were white women, and material aid was given where need was met. The school plant was adequate, the need very great and the workers earnest in their desire to do all in their power for the colored people.

There was a new principal at the school who was only just becoming acquainted with the neighborhood and the colored people, her work having been among the Jewish children on the lower East Side. She said the strongest characteristic of the colored children she had thus far discovered was their tendency to be guided by likes and dislikes for their teachers; that while it was possible to lead them to almost any extent, it was impossible to drive them.

Next to the Henrietta Industrial School of the Children's Aid Society, the most important plant in the San Juan Hill district is St. Cyprian's Parish House and Chapel, the former occupying three brownstone houses at 177–181 West 63rd Street. The work is in charge of the Rev. Joseph Johnson and Mrs. Johnson, with the assistance of a deaconness of the Episcopal church by whose mission St. Cyprian's work is supported.

The social activities of St. Cyprian's Parish House are distinct from those connected with the chapel, and included two features that seemed especially practical. One of these was a class in sewing for women and young girls the members of which were paid from five to fifteen cents an hour for their time while being taught. The garments made—plain, serviceable, comfortable underwear and children's clothing—were sold in the neighborhood at moderate prices and the proceeds of these sales supported the classes. The other activity was the maintenance of a model flat, furnished simply and in excellent taste, which was open every day in the week, Thursdays being devoted especially to housemaids who would otherwise have had no place to go on their afternoon off, and who had the privilege of writing letters, preparing supper, and dancing if anyone happened to be present who played the piano.

In the basement of the houses were a milk station and a laundry, the former open during the morning until noon. St. Cyprian's did not belong to the association of milk stations and was not employing the newest methods in vogue in the affiliated stations. The milk was prepared for the mothers purchasing it, instead of having the nurse in charge instruct and thereby educate the mother. It was felt that possibly the babies were given a better chance by using the older method, besides which, more money than St. Cyprian's could raise was necessary in order to join the association of milk stations.

A laundry was also installed in the basement with a large back yard, three houses deep, in which to hang the clothes. Mrs. Johnson said their laundry work came from patrons of St. Cyprian's parish who paid well to have their work done by hand and dried in the open air. In a neighborhood where there was such a dearth of playgrounds it seemed a pity to waste that back yard on drying clothes, but as the laundry furnished employment to a number of women at $1.00, $1.50 and $2.00 a day, and the profit from the work paid for cleaning and clerical help used in the parish house, the profit amounting to about $250 per year, such a use of the premises seemed unavoidable. The laundry was closed during the summer because all their patrons were out of the city at that time. They were hoping to secure funds with which to install modern appliances, as the laundry was quite primitive.

There was an employment bureau connected with the parish house, supplying mainly West Indian domestic help. It was stated that this work was carried on in quite an informal manner and no figures were available regarding the number of applicants or placements. There were also dressmaking, embroidery and cooking classes in charge of the wife of the pastor, a woman of tact and education with a most helpful attitude toward her work and the people she is working among.

St. Cyprian's Chapel has a good, completely equipped gymnasium, but it was being used by a comparatively small number of boys. Mr. Johnson said that he would welcome any boy, whether belonging to the parish or not; but the other social workers in the neighborhood said they had not found it possible to place their club boys there as a fee was demanded which the boys were unable to pay. The instructor furnished the year before by the Mission Society had just been withdrawn because of lack of response from the boys of the neighborhood.

Perhaps more than with any other race the life of the colored population centers around the church, and any movement for social betterment is far more apt to secure a hearing and consideration from the pulpit than in any other way. Settlement activities, whether or not they are connected with churches, kindergartens or day nurseries, make slow progress. It has been suggested that the democratic organization of social life among the colored people has contributed to this condition.

The Union Baptist Church, at 210 W. 63rd Street, is also an institutional church. Rev. George H. Sims, the pastor of this church, is an active force among the colored people of the district. There, as elsewhere, it was not possible to secure figures of attendance in social activities connected with the church, but it was stated that about 400 children attended the Sunday School regularly.

Rev. Victor G. Flynn, the white pastor of the Moravian church holding its services in the Children's Aid Society school building, is a keen student of the problems of the colored people. He said that the longer he lived among them the more firmly he was convinced that their cause was injured every time anything was done for them as colored people.

The Lincoln Day Nursery occupied the upper floor and the roof of the building at 202 West 63rd Street. There were accommodations for 79 children, but the average attendance was said to be from 25 to 35. The children two years old and younger were given a very simple luncheon and bread and milk at half-past nine in the morning and again at five in the afternoon. The older children had a more substantial luncheon, otherwise the food was the same. In other day nurseries cereal is usually given for breakfast and always milk for luncheon, as was not the case here.

The fee charged by the Lincoln Day Nursery was 10 cents per day for each child, or where there were three children in the family a charge of 25 cents for the three was made.

The usual fee in day nurseries for white children is said to be 5 cents a day for each child.

The nursery was well equipped and well cared for and the children were well kept, clean and most of them appeared well and happy. The Superintendent said that although they had 75 families on their register, the capacity of the nursery was very seldom taxed, as she did not take on new applicants and the mothers already registered worked on different days and so did not use the nursery at the same time.

She also said that the colored people of the neighborhood were for the most part self-respecting and hard-working but occasional lapses were found. She thought that it was significant that out of the 75 families on their list, they knew of only three in which there were illegitimate children. The day nursery did not refuse to take these illegitimate children when the mother's offense was a first one.

There was a Mothers' Club connected with the nursery, meeting once a month, and during the summer months the superintendent had charge of a summer home at Mt. Kisco, conducted under the auspices of the nursery.

The small number of families availing themselves of the day nursery privileges as contrasted with the accommodations provided, gave rise, naturally, to inquiries into the reason for this state of affairs, especially as one family after another was found later in which children were kept from school to care for their brothers and sisters below school age.

The difficulty, so far as could be learned from the very cursory inquiry made, was about equally divided between the hardship of paying the fee in families that were or should be receiving aid from relief-giving bodies, and personal feeling between mothers or older sisters and the maids at the nursery.

The New York Free Kindergarten and Clubs for Colored Children occupied the two lower floors of the building of the Lincoln Day Nursery, at 202 West 63rd Street. A branch of the music school settlement for colored people had been established in the Kindergarten building; also an amusement club for young women. Outings, circus parties, etc., were enjoyed by each club. The most cordial coöperation existed between this organization and the public schools in the vicinity. This coöperation consisted in inviting the colored children of the schools to participate in certain activities at the center, and in taking up neighborhood problems with the principals and teachers. No individual problems were, however, made the subject of coöperation; and even in this center—perhaps the most intelligently managed one among all the agencies for colored people—a number of children were found who had presented problems at their schools, and who, neither before nor after they were reported to the center, were given special consideration. One serious misunderstanding arose in school in the case of a girl belonging to one of the clubs in this center. The club was to have an outing, and this child, whose mother was not living, asked her father's permission to go to the park with her "teacher," as club leaders are commonly called by the children. Her father, an unusually careful parent, called at the school, learned there was to be no outing, and with the teacher accused the child of telling a falsehood. The girl had rather below the normal facility for expressing herself and could not explain satisfactorily. The matter was reported by the head of the department as an instance of flagrant untruthfulness. Later, in talking with the girl, the usual question was asked, if she belonged to any club. She eagerly said she did—to all of the clubs of the Free Kindergarten Association—and then the fact appeared that it was the "teacher" of this Club with whom she had asked permission to go to the outing, so the matter was cleared up with both teacher and father. How many small tragedies of this nature it is possible to avert— misunderstandings that may well affect a child's life—only the visiting teacher knows.

Miss Emerson, who had been in charge of the work of the Free Kindergarten since its inception, said she felt very strongly that an effort should be made to correlate the program of social activities in San Juan Hill with a view to having industrial training made the special feature of certain centers—say the Henrietta Industrial School and St. Cyprian's Parish House, while Stillman House and the Free Kindergarten Association, although not abandoning all their industrial work, might devote their programs to recreational and cultural activities.

Stillman House,* the colored branch of the Henry Street Settlement, reached an average of 500 persons each week in its social activities, 245 of these being depositors in the Penny Provident Fund.

Miss Wald stated that in her opinion the best work in connection with the house had been done, first, by the district nurses, and then by the men's and women's clubs. A class in manicuring and shampooing, taught by a thoroughly trained teacher, was well attended and diplomas were given to four of the twelve members, the other eight members forfeiting their diplomas because of irregular attendance.

During the summer of 1912 a successful playground out of doors was conducted by Stillman House with an average weekly attendance of about 475. The worker in charge was furnished by the City Department of Parks and Playgrounds and the children (who came in two groups, one from 9:30 to 12 o'clock A. M., and the second, from 2 to 5 o'clock P. M.) were required to remain until the close of the session. This ruling eliminated one of the most objectionable features of the school recreation centers, where the children were continually running in and out making program work almost impossible.

Probably about 1,500 persons were reached jointly by the social activities of the three centers, Stillman House, St. Cyprian's and the Free Kindergarten Association. There was said to be a colored population of 10,000 in the San Juan Hill district, and the school registers showed roughly about 1,200 children. It would therefore seem that a large percentage should have been represented in the clubs and other activities of these social agencies. The most careful inquiry failed, however, to indicate that such was the case; from the study of school children's amusements it appeared to be a very small one indeed. All the social

* See Appendix II.

agencies in the neighborhood seemed to be coöperating with the Henrietta Industrial School, but such coöperation apparently did not exist in the case of public schools in a district whose problems were many and varied.

Aside from the San Juan Hill district, activities for the betterment of colored people were studied in two other districts.

The first was that embraced in the territory of the Chelsea Neighborhood Association, extending from 34th to 42nd Street, and from Seventh Avenue to the North River. In this district are located Public Schools 28 and 32, each with a large proportion of colored children, but the only agencies for betterment were the Abyssinia Baptist Church, and two small missions, in neither of which were found any social activities for children. In this district, and especially in the immediate neighborhood of Public School 28, were some of the most vicious resorts for colored people as well as the greatest poverty.

The Colored Mission on West 30th Street is outside the district studied. It is doing an important work, and, among other activities, has a day nursery and classes in sewing and cobbling.

In Harlem, the second of these districts, between West 130th and 145th Streets, and Fifth and Eighth Avenues, new activities are added almost daily.

Two institutional churches—St. Philip's, Episcopal, and Salem Baptist—the Catholic Mission Church of St. Mark the Evangelist, and a chapel or mission literally on every block, provide for the social as well as the spiritual needs of their congregations, and indeed every colored church is in this respect more or less institutional. In no other place can as representative and intelligent an audience be obtained among the colored people as in their churches; and the church societies of men, women and children are identifying themselves with the most advanced methods of social progress. Discussions on the housing problem, promoted by the National League on Urban Conditions Among Negroes, were held in turn in all the large churches during the winter of 1912–13, and drew large and enthusiastic gatherings. Boy Scouts and Camp Fire Girls were being organized, the latter under the auspices of the Young Women's Christian Association. In a neighborhood house at 64 West 134th Street, devoted to mission work of the Cathedral of St. John the Divine, one of the finest women's meetings ever attended by the investigator was held in February, 1913. Miss Laura Garrett delivered a series of lectures on sex hygiene before the women's club, and on this particular evening the discussion by the women of the club showed intelligence and spiritual insight of a high order.

Interspersed with these sociological and ethical discussions were evenings devoted to every manner of activity, from "Old Maids' Conventions" to lectures by presidents of schools for colored people in the south, delivered for the purpose of securing financial aid for their work.

The societies connected with the Catholic mission churches of St. Benedict the Moor, on West 53rd Street, and St. Mark the Evangelist, on West 138th Street, gave artistically and financially successful performances of "Pinafore" during the spring and winter of 1913; and everywhere one finds, night after night, that the colored churches are free from the reproach of being useless from Sunday night to Sunday morning. If the various amounts contributed incessantly in five and ten cent pieces—even in pennies—at these meetings could be summed up, the resulting amount would undoubtedly be a most astonishing one.

One or two of the colored clergymen felt that the young people were breaking away from the church—that the temptations of dance halls and moving picture shows were proving more potent than their traditional Christian Endeavor Societies, Baptist Unions and St. Agnes Guilds of the Methodist, Baptist and Episcopal churches respectively; but the attendance at the meetings of these societies was large, and the interest of the young people seemed to be vital. The young men and young women as individuals devoted themselves to the work of the church, teaching in the Sunday Schools, assisting in church entertainments, etc., but as yet they have not made themselves felt as organizations. There is much fine material in these various bodies and it should not be difficult to stimulate them to helpfulness in larger social questions.

Opinions as to moral conditions in this section seemed to differ. One clergyman felt that the situation was very grave. He said that secret immoral resorts frequented by young boys and girls were in existence; and the neglect of parents to keep closely in touch with their children's amusements and companions was the cause of much trouble. On the other hand, another clergyman said he believed that the young people were doing very well indeed; and still another that he wondered they behaved as well as they did, so little encouragement was offered them.

St. Philip's Episcopal Church, not a mission, at 215 West 133rd Street, the rear of the church fronting on 134th Street, is said to be the richest colored congregation in the United States. The church is housed in a handsome brick structure designed by colored architects and built on institutional lines. Its pastor, Rev. Hutchins C. Bishop, is identified with most of the work being done for colored people in New York. He is a member of the executive board of both the National Association for the Advancement of Colored People and the League on Urban Conditions Among Negroes. St. Philip's Church has participated in all the discussions promoted by the League, and the congregation has supplied a number of Big Brothers who have taken a keen interest in the problems of school children. As a rule, however, these men are busy through long hours of work, and with every good intention can give only a limited amount of time to "Big Brothering" the neglected little ones they befriend.

In addition to the Sunday School and the church guilds of men and women at St. Philip's, there were senior and junior clubs, three for boys with a membership of about 80, and two for girls with a membership of 41, the lowest age for admission being 12 years for boys and 14 years for girls. There was also a gymnasium open six nights a week, the boys paying fifteen cents a month and the girls five cents a month. There was also a Boy Scout organization with a membership of 75.

Mr. I. W. Daniel, the assistant to the pastor of the church, and his wife were in charge of the social activities for the boys and girls. All these activities took place in the evening and the question was asked as to the advisability of afternoon activities, as well as the necessity of providing for the care in the afternoon of the younger children.

The pastor stated that this could not be done without an increased force as both Mr. and Mrs. Daniel were overtaxed. Besides this, it was always difficult to secure the attendance of girls and boys at afternoon clubs because of the many home duties, errands, etc., that devolved upon them. It appeared also that attendance in all the clubs was irregular and unreliable.

St. Philip's Church maintained an Old People's Home, and gave relief in form of monetary aid to meet insurance payments, rents, etc., the investigations being made by the pastor and his assistant. The Dorcas Society, composed of women members of the church, gave relief in the form of clothing, and on the recommendation of their committee, consisting of four members, funds in the pastor's custody were also disbursed. Mrs. Daniel said that relief was not limited to parish members. The church did not coöperate with the Charity Organization Society, nor did it register its cases with the Social Service Exchange. The statement was made that the investigations were very thorough and that there could be no overlapping in their cases.

St. Philip's was equipped with a billiard and smoking room, used by the men of St. Andrew's Brotherhood, and had half a dozen meeting rooms of different sizes in addition to offices, the gymnasium and a chapel extending through to West 134th Street. The congregation numbered about 1000, made up for the most part of working men and women, with a sprinkling of members of the professional class.

Mr. Daniel said St. Philip's principal need was $500 to equip their gymnasium, for which they had only a basket-ball outfit; also a piano for the gymnasium. A fund to purchase a piano had been started by contributions from the boys' and girls' clubs. The boys had practice for basket-ball in the recreation center at P. S. 89, and their track game practice at McCombs Dam. Mr. Daniel said, however, that the boys' clubs were not affiliated with the Athletic League. They had been members in years past, but their dues had not been paid and the membership had lapsed.

The girls' clubs, whose members range from 14 to 18 years old, were engaged in embroidery and drawnwork. They were also inaugurating the practice of giving entertainments for the inmates of the Old Ladies' Home. All the members of the clubs were school girls, excepting two who were dressmakers' assistants and who had graduated from the Washington Irving High School's dressmaking department.

The girls had a basket-ball club coached by a member of the boys' club. Their leader, Mrs. Daniel, said these girls were very domestic and helpful in their own homes, and that their clubs constituted the only amusement they had outside of their home circle. Mrs. Daniel herself is a graduate of Normal College and taught in the New York Public Schools before her marriage. She felt that the problem of street behavior was a serious one in the Harlem colored district, and said that she was most anxious about her own boys, who were approaching adolescence. Later in the winter, when taking part in the discussion of one of Miss Garrett's lectures on sex hygiene, she aroused much enthusiasm among the women present on the question of parents' duties to their boys in placing before them the problems involved in the relations of men and women.

Men and women of the type of these leaders in the social activities of St. Philip's could not fail to leave an impression on the lives of the young people associated with them. They were dignified and definite and left one feeling that if only a corps of volunteer workers were available for their needs they could develop a young people's social center which would be of great value in the community. Here, as elsewhere, however, it appeared that colored men and women of ability were so fully occupied with gainful employment and usually received so much smaller pay than did white workers of the same caliber that they could not afford to give their services without compensation. In each social center visited this same statement was made, and until the group of high school boys and girls was studied, the statement could not be contradicted. Among these boys and girls, however, was found the best sort of material for training as volunteer workers, and not only the material but also the spirit and wish to help.

Salem M. E. Church, also an institutional church, is located at 104 W. 133rd Street. The Rev. W. E. Cullen, pastor of the church, stated that the congregation was composed of about 700 men and women from laboring and professional classes, and that 350 children on an average attended the Sunday School. There were two boys' clubs, one junior and one senior, aggregating 75 to 80 members. The boys' clubs used the gymnasium in the church building on Monday, Tuesday and Wednesday evenings, seniors and juniors mixing on those nights. On other evenings the clubs met in their club rooms for parliamentary instruction, ethical discussions, games, etc. The work of the girls' clubs was not yet developed, but they met informally once or twice a week.

Mr. Cullen was deeply interested in the boys and girls of the neighborhood and appeared to be a vital influence with them. He was consulted a number of times concerning boys who presented social problems, and aided materially in securing evidence that helped place in jail at least two members of a gang of young men that had been a bad influence among the young girls of their neighborhoods.

According to his statements the streets east of Lenox Avenue were infested with gangs of young boys who were under the influence of older and hardened wrongdoers. He had reached the ring leaders of several of the gangs and had successfully held them in his boys' clubs.

He also spoke of the harm that had been done by loose women of the neighborhood, both colored and white, who enticed the more attractive colored boys into living lives of idleness supported by the earnings of these women. These boys, known in the neighborhood as "pimps," had adopted a uniform style of dress, consisting of a loose backed coat (they were also called "loose backs"), tight fitting trousers and tan shoes. They were an institution peculiar to the colored district, and at the time the investigation began could be found in twos and threes on almost every street corner. Mr. Cullen was informed by the investigator of the work being done by the Committee of Fourteen and placed in touch with Mr. Whitin, the general secretary. Since that time, as stated elsewhere, a number of immoral resorts in the neighborhood were closed, half a dozen notorious characters were jailed, and the "pimps" are no longer noticeable on the streets. They may be there, but they do not flaunt their profession by means of a uniform.

Mr. Whitin, of the Committee of Fourteen, said they would be glad to coöperate at all times in dealing with any phase of commercialized vice. Practically every case referred to them was sooner or later acted upon, either directly by them or by the Society for the Prevention of Cruelty to Children when boys and girls under sixteen were involved, as in the case of a former notorious "club" on West 30th Street. This was being used as a garage at the time of the investigation, but with the indecent mural decorations of the resort still untouched. A caretaker's family with three small children lived on the top floor, and within a week after the place was reported to the Committee of Fourteen, who in turn referred it to the Children's Society, the walls were repainted. Other cases learned of from the parents of school children and reported to these agencies have already been mentioned; still others are described in the statistical portion of the report and in Appendix I.

The Catholic Church is represented in the Harlem district by the chapel of St. Mark the Evangelist at 61 West 138th Street, in charge of Father Plunkitt; and by St. Mark's School at 50 West 134th Street. The chapel had between 500 and 600 families in its membership and the children from these families attended the Sunday School.

The social work with boys and girls was only just in process of development at St. Mark's chapel, but Father Plunkitt and the Brothers attached to the chapel were intimately acquainted with the families of both their colored and white parishioners, who were about equally divided as to race.

Among the activities there was a basket-ball court for boys, but no coach was provided for them. This court was used during the winter by the boys attending P. S. 100, who were too young to join the regularly organized basket-ball teams connected with their own congregations.

Father Plunkitt did not regard seriously the race disputes of the neighborhood and said that when he found two gangs engaged in an encounter he could scatter the boys with scarcely more than a word. The "White Rat" gang, composed of white boys in the vicinity of 138th Street and Fifth Avenue, and a gang of colored boys at the Lenox Avenue end of the block he found equally troublesome. Father Plunkitt thought that the police might be of more service in dealing with the situation if they merely scattered the boys whenever they were found congregated together, without paying too serious attention to their disputes. This seemed to him the right attitude.

The colored people of this parish, according to Father Plunkitt, were sober and industrious, with not nearly so high a percentage of shiftlessness and general troublesomeness as the corresponding element in the white population; and the attitude of some of the white people of the neighborhood, who objected to people infinitely their superiors merely because they were black was, he said, difficult to meet with patience.

In the Holy Name Society, the representative society of the Roman Catholic Church, Father Plunkitt said an effort had been made to maintain a mixed membership, but the colored people seemed to prefer to have their own society and to manage it themselves.

St. Mark's School was attended by about 125 boys and girls and supported by the Sisters of the Blessed Sacrament. The work of these sisters is with colored people and Indians, and in this Miss Katherine Drexel,—Mother Drexel, as she is known in the order—has been the moving spirit. The school is in charge of

Mother Paul, and in the fall of 1914 moved into its own building on 138th Street between Lenox and Fifth Avenues.

Mother Paul has a remarkable personality: vigorous, sweet, attractive and definite, and capable of exerting much firmness in enforcing discipline. She stated that wayward girls or boys were not retained among their pupils as they had found by experience that no improvement they were able to effect counteracted the bad influence exerted on the other children.

There were no formal social activities connected with the school, the Sisters in charge of the classes concerning themselves with problems affecting the morals, manners and lives in general of the families of their pupils.

Mother Paul said she had found that irregular attendance was apt to cover any sort of trouble. One of the girls who had not been coming regularly was discovered in Harlem Hospital, suffering from the effects of an abortion. This girl and her younger sister were asked to leave the school.

These girls were followed up by the investigator. They had gone to P. S. 119, where they had an unsavory record because of obscene notes they had written to other girls, and later had been sent to the Training School at Hudson through the efforts of the school nurse, who reported the case to the Children's Society.

St. Mark's School charged no fee to its pupils, but made a small charge for books, amounting to about fifty cents a year in the lower, and one dollar in the upper grades.

There are other churches, chapels and missions in the Harlem district; so numerous are they, in fact, that almost without exception between Seventh Avenue on the west and Fifth Avenue on the east, from 133rd to 135th Streets and from Lenox Avenue on the west on up to 140th Street, every block has from two to five organized congregations reflecting every shade of faith and nationality. The Danish West Indian has his chapel, as has also the West Indian from Barbadoes; while many of the ministers formerly in charge of formal congregations, but who for one reason or another had been deprived of or had left their parishes, have opened small independent "missions" that are more or less private and personal enterprises.

There were few philanthropic organizations in the district at the time the investigation began: The Hope Day Nursery, St. John's Home for Working Girls and the Milk Station of the Diet Kitchen Association. Since that time the Colored Branch of the Young Women's Christian Association has moved into Harlem.

The Hope Day Nursery occupied a four-story brownstone house at 114 West 133rd Street, and had been established for ten years. At the time the investigation began its capacity was enlarged, by permission of the Department of Health, from twenty-five to forty children. The matron in charge was also a member of the Board of Directors, who were all colored women. The matron said that the average attendance at the nursery was about 35. A charge of fifteen cents was made for each child cared for, two children in the same family being taken for twenty-five cents. This is the highest charge in any day nursery. The parlor floor, the only one visited by the investigator, was fairly well furnished and well kept. A mothers' club had recently been organized with an enrollment of twenty-seven members and at each monthly meeting a speaker was provided. Dr. E. R. Roberts, a colored physician, spoke at one meeting on the care of children. The investigator met with the club, by invitation, in February, 1913, and spoke to them on neighborhood problems. The matron was desirous of forming an auxiliary to the Nursery among the women of the neighborhood, as distinct from the Board of Managers. She thought that an auxiliary might help with the problems both of the Nursery and of the neighborhood, as there was no social work whatever connected with the Nursery. This plan, however, was not carried out in spite of continued planning and proffered coöperation, because the Board of Managers felt they were not warranted in undertaking any additional expense. The annual budget was already $2000, of which $1000 went for rent, and it was a hard struggle to gather this together. The suggestion was made that, since they had no other activities in the house, a smaller house, such as might be rented east of Lenox Avenue at about $700 a year, and which would be nearer poorer homes, might be preferable in view of the smaller outlay, both for rent and for upkeep.

The children of school age in the families registered at the Hope Day Nursery were permitted to have luncheon there, if desired, and to come there after school, but there were, as already stated, no organized social activities for these children and they were left to their own devices when they came. Seventeen children of school age from fourteen families were given after school

care.   The matron said she knew little about the families on their
list, as all details were left to the maids.

The work of the Music School Settlement, at 257 West 134th
Street, under the direction of Mr. David I. Martin, is coming to
be a potent factor in the lives of the colored people.   The headquarters are busy from the moment school closes until bed-time,
as well as the entire day on Saturday, with children's orchestra
rehearsals on Sunday afternoons.

The school was established by Mr. David Mannes in 1906, and
has grown steadily and healthily.   In the main school and the
branches maintained in the Free Kindergarten Association for
Colored Children, at 202 West 63rd Street, and in the New York
Colored Mission at 227 West 30th Street, upwards of 250 children
were being instructed in piano, violin, 'cello and ensemble playing.
The actual work performed in teaching may be termed, however,
merely the skeleton of the educational program of the settlement.   Its influence is felt in every institution in the city devoted to the interests of the colored people.   In the orphan
asylums at Riverdale and Kings Park, respectively, Mr. Martin
has maintained classes in vocal and orchestral music, and he is
continually busy preparing benefit performances for this or that
philanthropy.   When the principal of P. S. 89 asked where
he could secure talent for his Friday morning assemblies, he
was placed in touch with Mr. Martin, and the coöperation that
resulted brought definite returns, not only in the pleasure given
by the programs Mr. Martin furnished on various Friday morn-
ings, but in the influence on the development of the boys who
were referred to the Music School Settlement for instruction.

The Music School Settlement has made a dignified position for
itself in the community, and its concerts given at intervals in
Carnegie Hall, draw large and interested audiences.   The programs are devoted to the works of colored composers, interpreted by colored musicians.

Mr. Martin desired for Harlem a building that would not alone
house the Music School Settlement and provide an adequate
auditorium for its concerts, but would also serve as a center for
other social as well as more practical activities.   He felt that
the colored people should have a better amusement center than
was available for them.

The colored branch of the Young Women's Christian Association, at 121–125 West 132nd Street, was established in Harlem

during the period of the investigation, moving from its old quarters in West 53rd Street into three brownstone houses in a neighborhood only recently opened to colored people.

The work there followed closely the lines laid down for the Association's activities, and touched the problem of the school child only through its library and organization of Camp Fire Girls. The superintendent said that their educational program was decided upon from year to year. Their membership, recruited for the most part from housemaids, dressmakers, visiting maids, manicurists, hairdressers and that class of workers, made evening classes difficult, as much night work was performed by all the members.

The rear yards of the houses have been thrown together and fitted up for tennis and basket ball.

The older members of the Camp Fire Girls' circle were being drawn into the membership of the Association, and among these girls were found no members from the needier families. The girls were all from one social group, and appeared to have many social interests. Although these girls were receiving much help, they apparently made no return, and no community interest or social service on their part grew out of their connection with this branch of the Young Women's Christian Association. From individual instances known to the investigator material for some sort of social service might doubtless be found among the members of the Colored Young Women's Christian Association, even though it consisted of nothing more than waking and getting off to school the children of some working mothers. Even if this service were not rendered continuously, two weeks or a month devoted to instilling correct habits of rising and preparing for school might help. One small boy's attendance problem was solved by merely persuading his older sister, who had thought it of great importance to meet her girl friends and go to school with them, that her brother's prospective career as a truant was likely to lead to serious consequences and that it was her first duty to escort him to his school, which did not happen to be the same one she attended.

The possibility of coöperating with the school for the purpose of rendering some form of assistance in working out the children's problems was suggested to the superintendent, who said she would endeavor to work out a program along that line.

The sole milk station of the colored district of Harlem, that of the Diet Kitchen Association at 27 West 139th Street, had, in addition to its regular milk station activities, organized a mothers' club with the aid of the social worker from the Free Kindergarten Association. This worker felt that a day nursery was also greatly needed in this neighborhood, which was made up of thickly populated tenements of medium grade.

One of the most illuminating incidents of the investigation was connected with this milk station. A tuberculous baby girl was discovered in one of the families visited and the mother was sent to the milk station to have the baby's weight carefully watched, as well as to secure for both mother and baby the material and educational privileges of the station. The woman became enthusiastically interested in the nurse's counsel and in keeping a record of the baby's progress, and knew to the fraction of an ounce its gain or loss. During the spring the baby had whooping cough, which she transmitted to one of the older children in the family—a child of six. In June, on going in to learn how both children were getting along, the visitor found them still coughing, and on that particular afternoon entertaining about fifteen of their friends in celebration of the baby's second birthday! The mother was so proud and happy it seemed impossible to scold her then, but afterwards she was asked why she had exposed all those children to the whooping cough. She said they might have caught it anywhere, and added that she was sure that the baby had contracted it at the milk station because that was the only place she went, excepting to walk or to the moving pictures!

When the agent of the Harlem branch of the Charity Organization Society was consulted as to social conditions in this section, she said family relations were in such a confused and tangled condition among the colored people that she could find little upon which to base family reconstruction. In her opinion, the Society for the Prevention of Cruelty to Children was infinitely more needed than the Charity Organization Society, as most of the children in families brought to her notice required other guardianship before a constructive program for their future welfare could be worked out. Applications to the Charity Organization Society for assistance were increasing rapidly from the colored population, and while help was undoubtedly needed, it was apparent that other readjustments were equally necessary. At that time a list of representative colored people who might coöperate with this branch of the Charity Organization Society and perhaps form a colored neighborhood advisory board, was given the agent, and after several months they were asked to meet with her to form a class for the study of relief work.

The district east of Lenox Avenue, and running to the East River, from 131st Street on the south to 142nd on the north, contained the poorest and neediest of the Harlem Negroes. Aside from the smaller and less important churches and missions (excepting the two on 138th Street) there were no social agencies whatever, and cheap dance halls run by private clubs, some of them in tenement basements, flourished.

It is the almost universal custom in this section for every adult member of the family not incapacitated by age to go out to work; and in one home after another the children were found to be either alone after school or in the charge of an aged grandmother, sometimes an efficient guardian but more often incapable of understanding conditions or remedying them if she did understand them.

St. John's Home for Working Girls at one time made an effort to establish settlement activities in its 134th Street house, but the home has since moved to 132nd Street, west of Lenox Avenue, into a less needy neighborhood.

There are said to be sixty thousand colored people in Harlem between 130th and 142nd Street, Park Avenue on the east, and Eighth Avenue, Seventh Avenue or Lenox Avenue on the west, according to whether the blocks beyond have been opened to colored tenants or not. It is difficult to estimate adequately the work done in this section by the small missions and churches. If it were not for their ministrations, both spiritual and physical, Harlem Negroes would fare badly.

RECREATIONS, PRIVATE AND PUBLIC

The most salient point developed by the study of the social agencies was the apparent lack of response to any activity that was not founded on a real and practical need. Boys' and girls' clubs had not generally been successful; classes were very moderately successful; and day nurseries did not seem to be filled to their capacity at any time. Parents appeared not to be enthusiastic about the possibilities of clubs, especially for girls; and the interest of both boys and girls did not hold, except in the case of one or two brigades of Boy Scouts and the chapter of Camp Fire Girls which was made up entirely of girls coming from a superior type of home.

Irregular attendance at clubs and classes is the subject of general complaint by social workers among the colored people. It is not difficult usually to secure a good audience for special meetings that have been well advertised, but for week in and week out activities the interest must be more than ordinarily deep to hold any large number, whether men, women or children. The colored people do not take their recreations seriously. A club to them is a staple form of amusement available every week, which logically gives way to a ball, a "social," or an evening at the theater. It would be difficult to make them understand that there is any virtue in regular attendance at an activity of that nature; and in discussing the matter with them from the standpoint of the club leader, who must be present and who sets aside the time regularly, the almost invariable response has been in effect: "Yes'm; but the meetings is for pleasure and may be jest that evenin' our pleasure is somewhere else."

In two of the centers the question of poor attendance in the girls' clubs took on a more serious aspect. One of the head-workers followed up the absences, and found the girls, who had never before been allowed to go out of the house in the evening, had taken advantage of the unwonted liberty to go to a dance-hall. When this was reported to the parents they were naturally angry and refused to permit the girls to go out again in the evening.

In the other case, the parents said they allowed the girls to go to an evening center across the street from their flat, watching them from the window until they entered the building in which the club met. It was learned that the girls were accustomed to go to the club, remain there a few moments, and then leave and go to other places of which their parents knew nothing.

This raised the question—which has been since discussed by the workers among colored boys and girls—of the desirability of evening clubs, for young girls especially. None of the school principals who were consulted favored evening clubs but they believed that school girls should have their recreation after school, devoting the evening to study and early retiring.

Few of the parents approved of the clubs at all, whether afternoon or evening; and the carefully brought up girls who did belong to social clubs, or took part in church entertainments, were accompanied by either a relative or woman friend. Even the younger members of the Camp Fire Girls, organized under the auspices of the Young Women's Christian Association, were accompanied to meetings by parents or by other older women.

When asked what they thought about the desirability of afternoon clubs and other social activities in the schools, there was almost unanimous approval on the part of parents; but although settlement clubs and classes were recommended whenever children were found who had no such connection and who appeared to be in need of it, a card of introduction to the head worker of the settlement given the mother and the nature of the work fully explained, not one instance was found in which such a connection had been made.

It has been often said that in their public amusements the colored people are restricted to shabby, badly kept resorts where questionable, if not actually degrading, performances are offered.

Every moving picture and vaudeville theater in the colored districts was visited on a number of occasions, and taking them as a whole they offer attractions equal to those shown in any of the white neighborhoods known to the investigator. These theaters have come into existence only during the past few years; and on Seventh Avenue, 135th Street and Lenox Avenue there are eight well-kept, well-lighted, decently managed moving picture houses, the Lafayette, Seventh Avenue and 131st Street, leading in the attractiveness and variety of its program. Educational features, such as moving pictures of the National Colored Men's Business Association, with Booker T. Washington and other colored men of national reputation, historical scenes of interest to colored people, and a vaudeville bill that earned for itself a special article in the Sunday World have made this the leading amusement place in Harlem for colored people. It would be difficult to imagine a more decent, more responsive, and better pleased audience than one finds in this theater. An especially popular organization, the Colored Players, has appeared several times in this theater, and its members might develop with very little guidance into definitely artistic portrayers of the life of their own people. This theater building also contains a dance hall, the only one of its kind, open to the colored public each night. In the colored community dances have taken the form of balls given under the auspices of one social organization or another, varying in character with the organization giving them. The Lafayette dance hall is, however, a new venture and promises to be a successful one.

The Odd Fellows Hall, on West 138th Street, between Fifth and Lenox Avenues, has an excellent auditorium, and is much used for concerts and entertainments. Young's Casino, at 134th Street and Fifth Avenue, and the Manhattan Casino, 155th Street and Eighth Avenue, are much used for concerts, balls, basket-ball matches, etc.

The athletic contests between the teams of various churches, colleges, settlements, etc., are usually followed by some form of social gathering, and constitute the healthiest, sanest, as well as, happily, the most popular form of amusement of the well-brought-up young people. No one attending them could doubt the genuineness of the pleasure they afford their audiences. It might safely be said that Harlem, at any rate, offers much that is definitely good to the colored young people in the way of amusements. Downtown, aside from the settlements and churches, there is nothing of value, however. The moving pictures are poor and the vaudeville houses offer nothing worth while. In fact, in the immediate San Juan Hill neighborhood there was not at the time of the investigation a moving picture house of any kind, good or bad.

In none of these districts were enough forms of social activity found during these preliminary visits to account for the recreation of any large number of children of school age and only through the intensive study of school cases were the definite needs discovered.

Part II

INTENSIVE STUDY

I. Neighborhood Conditions

In the intensive study made, following the preliminary survey of general conditions, three districts were included: Harlem, San Juan Hill, and the Chelsea District between 34th and 42nd Streets—districts quite as different in general character and composition as though they constituted three distinct and separate cities.

The Harlem colored district lies roughly between 130th and 145th street, extending for the most part from Eighth Avenue to the East River. Certain blocks—136th and 141st to 145th— have few or no homes open to colored people between Lenox and Eighth Avenues, but from Lenox Avenue east to Park Avenue and to the Harlem River, there is little or no restriction against colored tenants. From 130th to 132nd Street, between Lenox and Seventh Avenues, is found the best part of the district— brown stone houses, varying from medium to poorer grade, with an occasional sprinkling of the better class house. This district continues up Lenox Avenue from 130th to 145th Streets.

Property values in this section have declined, as is usually the case when streets are given up to colored residents. Fifteen different real estate agents who were questioned on this point could give no reason for the decline. On the other hand they acknowledged that colored people paid higher rents than did white tenants in the same houses; that they kept the houses in quite as good repair as did the white people who formerly lived in them; and the Suburban Homes Company, owning two model tenements, the Hampton and Tuskegee, on West 63rd Street (for colored people only) said that these tenements were kept in better order, rents were paid more promptly and less trouble was experienced by removals, than in any of the other three groups of tenements owned by the same company in other parts of the city, and occupied by white tenants.

At the time of the investigation, banks and title guarantee

companies had been for over a year refusing to renew mort-
gages on property in colored districts.   It is impossible to say
how far this was one of the manifestations of the much talked of
real estate panic, but it has not tended to improve the temper of
the Harlem Board of Trade, which has been unfriendly to the
influx of colored population and has fought inch by inch every
gain in territory by colored tenants, especially in the direction
of the better neighborhoods.   In the blocks adjoining those in
which colored people lived, brownstone house after brownstone
house bore a sign, "To Let" or "For Sale."

From Fifth Avenue east, in some instances to Park Avenue,
in others to the East River, and from 130th to 145th Streets,
are the poorer class of flat houses and tenements; in some blocks
white and colored are mixed.   On Lenox Avenue itself, a
number of high grade apartment houses have been opened to
colored tenants and are for the most part filled with colored
people of the professional classes, one or two of the houses,
however, being in ill-repute.   One hundred and thirty-fourth
and 136th Streets between Lenox and Fifth Avenues are particularly given over to "Buffet" flats, so-called because liquor
is illegally sold in these places.   They are also, in the majority
of cases, disorderly resorts.   Rents vary from $12.00 for a three-
room unheated flat to $60 and $70 for six- and seven-room elevator apartments.   The medium priced houses rent for about
the same as houses of their class in like white districts, i. e.,
$18–$20 for a four-room steam-heated apartment of the new
law type; $26 and $28 for five- and six-room apartments of
the "railroad" flat or type of flat having no private hall, etc.
There was much complaint from tenants of poor heating and lack
of attention to the collection of garbage.   The streets were in
fairly good condition, but there was considerable violation of the
ordinance against placing garbage and refuse on the streets in
packages.   This was not nearly so noticeable, however, as in the
East Side tenement districts.

The district was well-lighted but poorly patrolled and between
Lenox and Madison Avenues an officer was seldom found.   On
one occasion the investigator walked about for three-quarters of
an hour before finding a patrolman.

The shops are ubiquitous, and there is not a block in any part
of the district that does not boast at any rate an undertaker's
or a caterer's establishment.

From Seventh Avenue to Fifth Avenue, the shops on 135th Street represent every variety of trade, with poolrooms, barber shops and restaurants predominating. The restaurants are unusually inviting. The tables are spotlessly clean and the service and food excellent.

A real estate office, handsomely furnished, is manned completely by a colored staff, from the proprietor to the office boy. A large and growing furniture business has been established. Lawyers, doctors, dentists have offices between Lenox and Seventh Avenues. There are grocery stores, dry goods and millinery shops, corsetiers, milliners and dressmakers, custom tailors and undertakers.

The National League on Urban Condition Among Negroes has its Harlem headquarters in this block, in which the work of its housing and employment bureaus is carried on.

But over and above all, located everywhere and anywhere in this and other colored districts, is the hair-dressing-massage-bath industry carried on by the colored women—the "Beauty Parlors" of the race. More will be said of this industry in the chapter devoted to occupations. (See pp. 120–121.)

In the block between Lenox and Fifth Avenues are the pool and billiard rooms, and moving picture and vaudeville theatres, with more grocery stores, restaurants, etc., but of a cheaper grade than those in the block farther west.

Following is a list of the shops on three blocks: 134th Street between Lenox and Seventh Avenues; east side of Seventh Avenue between 134th and 135th Streets and 135th Street between Lenox and Seventh Avenues. The list shows also the shops owned or operated by white people. It was not possible to secure any information concerning the amount of capital represented by or invested in these shops.

BUSINESS ENTERPRISE

One Hundred and Thirty-fourth Street, between Lenox and Seventh Avenues

South side of street, starting at Lenox Avenue

Butcher (store)....................................White
Tailor (store)....................................... "
Laundry (store)..................................... "
Barber shop (store)..............................Colored
Grocery (store)...................................White
Shoemaker (store)................................. "
Grocery (store)..................................... "
Employment Agency (in flat house)................Colored
Restaurant (basement flat house)................... "

Tailor (flat)......................................Colored
Expressman (flat)................................. "
Laundry (flat).................................... "
Ice and coal and shoe shine (basement flat house) ..... "
Minister (sign stating "Funerals–Marriages")........ "
Dressmaker (flat)................................ "
Restaurant (in basement).......................... "
Shoemaker and shoe repairing (in basement).......... "
Ice, coal and wood (basement in flat house)........... "
Milliner (flat)................................... "
Milliner (also piano teacher) (flat).................. "
Tailor (basement—cor. Seventh Ave.)................White

North side of street, starting at Lenox Avenue

Cigars and stationery (store).......................White
Restaurant (store)..............................Colored
Hairdressing, etc. (flat)........................... "
Tailor (flat)..................................... "
Jeweller (West Indian) (flat)....................... "
Dressmaker (flat)................................ "
Shoe repairing (basement in flat)................... "
Ice and coal (basement in flat)..................... "
Hairdressing, manicuring, etc. (flat)................. "
Florist (flat).................................... "
Notion store.................................... "
Hairdressing, facial massage, manicuring, etc. (flat).... "
"Church of God " (in flat house)................... "
Piano studio (in flat house)........................ "
Dressmaker (in flat house)......................... "

(Eight furnished room signs were found in the block, including both sides of the street.)

Seventh Avenue, between 134th and 135th Streets, East side of street, starting at corner 134th St.

Ice cream parlor and tea room (store)................Colored
Pool room (store)................................ "
Barber shop (store)............................... "
Barber shop (store)............................... "
Undertaker (store)............................... "
Laundry (store)..................................White
Ready-to-wear women's clothing (store).............. "
Furs (store)..................................... "
Restaurant (colored patrons) (store)................. "
Fur shop (store).................................. "
(Colored fur operator employed, earning $9.50 per week)
Drug store......................................White

One Hundred and Thirty-fifth Street between Lenox and Seventh Avenues South side of street, starting at corner 7th Ave.

Shoe shop (store)................................White
Hat cleaner (store)............................... "
Tailor (store).................................... "
Dentist (flat)...................................Colored
Graduate nurses' home (flat)....................... "
Hairdressing, shampooing, scalp treatment (flat)....... "
Electric massage machines (flat).................... "
N. Y. News (flat)................................ "
Dressmaker (flat)................................ "
Real estate (flat)................................ "
Real estate (flat)................................ "
Employment Agency (flat).......................... "
Lawyer (flat).................................... "

Hairdresser and dressmaker (flat)..................Colored
Jewelry and novelties (flat).......................   "
Milliner (flat)....................................   "
Saloon (store)....................................White
Restaurant (store)................................Colored
Merchant tailor (store)............................   "
Grocer (store)....................................White
Tailor (store)....................................   "
Grocer (store)....................................   "
Barber (store)....................................Colored
Saloon (store) ....   "
Restaurant (double store).........................   "
Delicatessen (store)..............................White
Coal and wood (store, basement)...................Colored
Candy and cigars (flat)...........................   "
Barber shop (basement and flat)...................   "
Hairdresser (flat)................................   "
Lunch stand (store)...............................   "
Painter (store)...................................White
Second-hand furniture (store).....................Colored
Real estate (store)...............................White
Barber shop (store)...............................Colored

North side of street, starting at 7th Ave.

Real estate (double store)........................Colored
Plumber and Printer (store).......................White
Tailor (West Indian) (store)......................Colored
　　(Tailor states that he employs white operators, because he finds it difficult to secure colored workers.)
Cigars (double store).............................Colored
Tailor (double store).............................   "
Dressmaker (double store).........................   "
Advertising Agency (double store).................   "
Stationery (double store).........................White
Furniture (double store)..........................Colored
Grocery (double store)............................White
Undertaker (double store).........................Colored
Harlem Branch Urban League........................   "
Laundry supply (store)............................   "
New York News (store).............................   "
Stationery (store)................................White
Teas and coffee (store)...........................Colored
Furniture (two double stores).....................   "
Grocer (store)....................................White
Undertaker (store)................................Colored
Music (store).....................................   "
Barber shop (store)...............................   "
Shoe-shine (store)................................   "
Custom tailor (store).............................White
Real estate and insurance (store).................Colored
Market (store)....................................White
Milliner (store)..................................Colored
Dresser (store)...................................White
Family liquor (store).............................   "
Grocer (store)....................................Colored
Shoe-shine (store)................................White
Bakery and groceries (double store)...............Colored
Dry goods (store).................................White
Laundry (store)...................................   "
Dry goods (double store)..........................   "
Electric contractor (store).......................Colored
Shoe-shine (store)................................   "

The Harlem District, aside from the fact that the houses are tenement houses, might be a colored village so far as its outward characteristics are concerned. The sociability of groups on the streets, the general informality of life and the close community of interests and social relationships of the families living in the tenements have little that is typical of New York about them. The cosmopolitan character of the district becomes apparent when one finds a newly arrived family from the West Indies eagerly and perilously hanging out of fourth story windows to view the strange street life of their adopted city, one mother saying that her four-year-old son's especial admiration was the "box full of music that comes around on four wheels every day." From one apartment come the strains of a Bach fugue being practiced by the daughter of an established merchant of the neighborhood, who is fitting herself to teach music. Still another few steps discloses a front stoop alive with children and a bandanaed "Auntie" fresh from the South. Sandwiched among these is the New York Negro family, thoroughly and typically American in its mode of life and ideals.

Harlem, as previously stated, has had few purely social agencies. The normal every-day life of the people centers about the home, work, the church and public amusements, the two latter providing most of the social life of the community. Public amusements: moving picture theatres, public halls, etc., are multiplying quickly, and shop-windows are crowded with handbills announcing entertainments furnished by every sort of colored organization, from a basket-ball contest between Howard University of Washington, D. C., and a local team, to a dance or a picnic by independent social organizations.

In spite, therefore, of its dearth of settlements and other organized philanthropic activities, Harlem cannot be said to lack amusement facilities for its adult colored population, nor are these facilities, as indicated in the preliminary survey, of a character to be despised.

The children are not so fortunate. Aside from the public library and the "movies" there is little for their pleasure. In summer a few badly regulated and itinerant carousel shows establish themselves in the unoccupied open lots of the neighborhood. During the summer of 1914 a trial of the suggestion made in another part of this report, that these vacant lots be equipped with playground apparatus, was inaugurated. There is no park space and no playground except in one public school; this has never been well organized and is given over, in the main, to practice by the various basket-ball teams of the neighborhoods.

In spite of this dearth of organized amusement for children, or perhaps because of it, in this district as well as in the others visited a more normal social life was found among most of them —a normal, social enjoyment of visits exchanged informally among friends, "taffy-pulls," etc.—than the investigator had observed in any other tenement population. After-school visiting was the rule among little girls who were friends and whose parents were not too busy to permit this form of amusement. The children of poorer working parents were, as a rule, however, not thus fortunate. These children either played upon the streets without any care, or were instructed by their parents to remain indoors, busy with household tasks or with the preparation of lessons. In some cases it was impossible to secure entrance to an apartment, although the children had been seen at the school, so strictly had they been ordered to open the door to nobody. Both this strict care on the one hand and the lack of care on the other were found to arrest development in the child, and instance after instance of the lack of means of self-expression was noted among these children who go through life from day's end to day's end without companionship, their parents having no knowledge of what their thoughts are, to say nothing of properly guiding those thoughts. It is no wonder that numerous cases of backwardness develop at the age of twelve or fourteen years; or that the scale of conduct and mentality does not show a larger proportion of high grade children.

Scattered through the district, but especially in the blocks between Lenox and Fifth Avenues, on 134th and 136th Streets, were the "Buffet" flats previously mentioned. In visiting the homes of school children on these blocks, however, less than half a dozen flats were found in which there were any evidences of irregularities of this nature. A number of colored people when asked about this stated that few children had been seen in the "Buffet" flats by anyone familiar with them.

As this description shows, Harlem is a normal community with a normal community's good, bad and indifferent features. San Juan Hill, on the other hand, is by blocks philanthropic or neglected slum in character; and the population seems to divide itself between the "up-lifters" and those to be or in process of being up-lifted. The community institutions, shops, stores, etc., have no relation to the neighborhood itself, and are not owned or operated by the colored people. The stores are for the most part on the Avenue and there is nothing characteristic about them. Here and there a small business owned by colored people is springing up tentatively on the edge of a block, giving one the impression of being ready to pick up its skirts and disappear on slight provocation; but the characteristic portion of the neighborhood is made up of model tenements erected by philanthropists; of settlements and other agencies for social betterment; and of mission churches for the most part philanthropically supported.

Directly across the streets from the model tenements, however, tenements were found with stairs in such dangerous condition that the visitor was almost precipitated from roof to cellar on several occasions; and many statements were made by women of the neighborhood that they had been received at police stations where they had gone to make complaints of neighborhood disorder as though they, themselves, were criminals.

Aside from the Public Recreation Center between 10th and 11th Avenues and 59th and 60th Streets, there is no form of amusement in the immediate neighborhood, except those connected with social agencies. There are no moving picture houses and no theatres nearer than 8th Avenue and 59th Street or Broadway.

Rents in this district vary from $8 to $10 for three rooms unheated, to $16 and $18 and even $24 a month for steam-heated four-room-and-bath flats in model tenements.

In the district farther downtown, between 34th and 42nd Streets and between 53rd and 59th Streets, the former section lying within the boundaries of the Chelsea Neighborhood Association, the most heterogeneous population imaginable lives together, sometimes in the same house, always in the same block. All the tenement houses are old-fashioned and the majority of them are dilapidated. Rents vary from $8 to $12 in the unheated houses to $16 and $20 in those supplied with steam heat, the latter, however, being rare. The colored population, mixed as it is with Greek, Armenian, Jew and Italian, is in its speech and manners distinctively, one is tempted to say "Cockney" New York. It should be explained, perhaps, that by "Cockney" New York one means the New York of Chimmie Fadden and his ilk. This population has none of the accepted characteristics of the

Negro, and if not its occupations, at any rate its interests are in sports of one sort or another. Families live here year after year and are almost as much a part of the neighborhood as the buildings themselves. The sprinkling of new-comers stays but a short time and school records show an almost constant transfer to either the San Juan Hill or the Harlem locality.

The only agency for colored people in this neighborhood is the Abyssinia Baptist Church between Seventh and Eighth Avenues. There are no clubs and classes, however; only the Young People's Society for Christian Endeavor and the Sunday School. The congregation, for the most part, lives out of the district.

There are two colored missions below 34th Street. The ministers in charge are representative colored men interested in everything concerning the development of their race. They have, however, organized no social activities for young people, and while a few of the boys and girls attend the New York Colored Mission's clubs and classes, the location of this mission on West 30th Street is too far downtown to affect the pupils of the school on West 40th Street.

Home conditions were alike in Harlem, San Juan Hill and the Chelsea districts in spite of the dissimilarity of these districts in other respects.

In the families visited, the much-talked-of "Lodger" problem was found to be, after all, not so much of a problem. Few of the families in which there were no male members received male lodgers. When the mother was a widow, her lodgers were invariably women. Far from being the virtue-devouring ogres they were supposed to be, the lodgers, as a rule, took a lively interest in the children's school progress; and many times on visiting the homes these same lodgers were found helping the children with their lessons. On more than one occasion the lodgers admonished the children to be careful about telling the truth and assisted their memories from time to time, when the children themselves could not recall matters about which inquiries were made.

Eight boys and four girls had no companionship whatever except the lodgers in their homes who worked at night, every member of the immediate family going to work during the day.

Undoubtedly there is danger from lodgers, but in the majority of cases it seems only fair to assume that this danger may be quite as much due to carelessness of parents in choosing the calibre of their lodgers as to any inherent evil in admitting lodgers to the family. Instances have occurred of the betrayal of girls by trusted friends lodging in the family, but they have also occurred under other conditions. Undoubtedly lodgers eke out incomes that in many cases would otherwise be inadequate to support life.

A very real and ever present danger was found to lurk in unoccupied flats, roofs and basements of tenement houses. The majority of cases of sex immorality of school children encountered in the course of the investigation or heard of from other sources, had been made easier of accomplishment because of the availability of one or all of these three places. Danger from places of this sort is very hard to guard against. Immoral resorts regularly carried on in furnished rooms, "bachelor apartments," etc., may be placed under police surveillance more easily than the above mentioned places.

Homes of every variety were found, and in both atmosphere and physical condition they reflected every shade of character and expression that belongs to families who live in New York and send their children to the public schools. Tasteful furnishings, quiet colors, well-chosen pictures and an air of comfort in some houses contrasted with other homes containing broken furniture and giving a general impression that someone had assembled all the family possessions in the centre of the floor and then tossed them haphazard to the four corners of the apartment. Between these two extremes lay solidly, and in the great majority, the typical fittings of the installment-furniture-house "five-rooms-complete-for-$————," invariably accompanied by a brass bed-stead, and very generally by a piano.

The greatest surprise of the whole investigation was encountered in a dilapidated tenement in the West Forties—the only house that seemed dangerous to enter because dusk was falling and the family to be visited lived on the fourth floor. The girl who lived there had been reported by her teacher "backward of understanding and uncertain of temper," and the dark, rickety stairs were climbed with many misgivings. The apartment was a poor three-room affair with bed-rooms partitioned off by hangings; but in one corner was a new piano of excellent make.

While talking with the girl and with her mother (both of whom were apparently below average in every way), the girl was asked if she cared for music, a question prompted by the presence of the piano. She said that she did not, but that her older sister had graduated from the Washington Irving High School three years previously and had been unable to find employment as a stenographer and bookkeeper, for which occupation she had been trained. Her ambition was not to be killed, however, and she had become a chambermaid in a small west-side hotel, devoting all her leisure time to the study of the piano. "She's got two years more," her mother said, "and nobody ain't going to boss her no more. No Ma'am; that girl, she calculated she's going to be something."

The girl was asked during the visit if she had thought of any occupation she would care to follow, and her mother chimed in with "Now, Miss, it's like this. You knows and I knows we all aint got the same kind of brains; and L. here, she got just plain house-keepin' brains. She aint like her sister. No Ma'am."

And so the homes, some planned with fine taste, some decorated with gay paper flowers, chromos and plush furniture, and still others, the expression of "just plain housekeepin' brains."

In all of the homes of the better type there was a striking prevalence of pictures with the Maxfield Parrish and Jules Guerin coloring. So general was this type of picture as to be almost startling; and these homes finally grouped themselves in the mind of the visitor, as of the "Parrish type." The rich tones and Oriental or mediæval subjects evidently appeal strongly to the love of form and color that is so strong a characteristic of the Negro race. In this type of home, the pictures formed a background for furniture usually of the mission style, with simple liberty curtains and hangings at the windows and doors. The men who supported these homes were lawyers, railroad employees, chauffeurs, musicians, chefs, porters, etc., while the women, who in many cases bore no small share of the cost of maintenance, were dressmakers, steamboat stewardesses, theatre and department store maids, lunch-room cooks, etc.

But orderly or slovenly, tasteful or garish, comfortable or squalid, there is found in the majority of colored homes a spirit of home-making and of what is expressed only by the German "*gemüthlichkeit*," and by no word in any other language. A big, bare kitchen at the top of a tenement house, the back door open, letting in a flood of sunshine with a cat basking in its warmth, while within a little group of girls sit about a table and chatter, and one is greeted by the small hostess and introduced to "my little friends." Another kitchen, filled with newly washed clothes, soapsuds, unwashed dishes and a large perspiring mater familias. Tucked into the corner of a big rocking chair, a small brown brother, his head drooping on one shoulder, pessimistically surveys the visitor. An inquiry whether the baby is ill, brings a hearty: "Lord no, Miss, he all ain't sick. He's 'ceitful, he is. He's jest takin' you in." Or one is ceremoniously led to a living room, to discuss the affairs of the child or children in whose behalf the visit is made, and usually the entire family, including lodgers, interestedly survey the problems in hand.

The frequency with which parents and children were found reading the Bible together when calls were made on Sunday, bore still further testimony to the very real part religion plays in the Negroes' lives. A discussion of the previous Sunday's sermon was often found to be the topic of conversation when a call coincided with that of other visitors.

On the other hand, in some of the homes a sideboard laden with every variety and size of drinking glass was the most conspicuous article of furniture; and card parties were frequently interrupted.

In a rear fourth-story room a little child was found battling for life with pneumonia. Her labored breathing mingled with the snores of a drunken father stretched across the foot of the bed. Her eyes were glazed in semi-consciousness but her tiny, hot hand held fast to a pitiful paper bag of candy. The elderly neighbor in charge, who was endeavoring to give the patient a drink of ginger ale, said that the mother, the sole support of the family, was away at work. The child had not been sent to a hospital because "if the baby died her mother wanted to feel that she had done everything she could."

The number of men on the street and at home during the day was a puzzling matter, as it had been to the school nurse; and it was not until a résumé of the occupations of these men showed how much night work they performed as railroad porters, chauffeurs, elevator men, longshoremen, tunnel laborers, etc.,—that their presence resolved itself largely into a question of night employment, rather than of unemployment.

To what extent the marriage tie bound the parents of the children visited cannot be stated with any degree of accuracy. By their own statements six mothers were divorced and six had never been married. The homes in which the children of these women lived varied as widely in character as did the calibre of the women themselves. From intelligence and industry to ignorance and indolence, they ran the gamut in the scale of human equipment.

V. J., 13 years old, in 6-B grade, showed no trace of color, had charming manners, an agreeable personality and every mark of good home training. Her father was a white man to whom her mother had not been married. The five-room flat in which she lived was plainly and comfortably furnished, and V. was a member of a large colored church congregation, was active in Sunday School affairs and enjoyed the affection of her playmates.

The Society for the Prevention of Cruelty to Children had separated V. from her mother two years previously, and had sent her to Boston to attend school. "I missed mother so much, though," V. said ingenuously, "that I just couldn't study. We couldn't bear to be away from each other, and when I came back to New York, I was way back in my studies." Whenever V. was called upon after school, she invariably was found busy with household tasks: mending, music lessons, and other homely occupations.

Under threat of a second separation by the Society of Prevention of Cruelty to Children, V.'s mother, who was a housemaid, finally consented to marry the man with whom she was living; and the last word received of V. was a message from her mother that V. was no longer to be registered as V. J. in school, but that she would take her step-father's name of F————. Mrs. F. bitterly resented interference with her private affairs; and said that if V. had been neglected,—"if she was not being brought up like a little lady"—such interference might be warranted.

G. B., 12 years old, in 5B grade, was found, on visiting her home, washing dishes while her mother sewed on a little dress for the immaculately kept baby sprawling on the floor. Mrs. M. gave her husband's occupation as porter in a downtown office building. A few moments later she stated that G.'s father was in Jamaica and the inquiry if he was on a vacation brought the explanation in quite a matter of fact manner, and in G.'s hearing, that her husband was not G.'s father to whom she had never been married. "I was engaged to him and the wedding invitations had been sent out, when I found out he was a gambler; and of course I wouldn't marry a worthless man like he was," she said. When the hope was expressed that good care would be taken of G. so she would not make a like mistake, "No indeed," Mrs. M. replied, "I was brought up very strict, and I am just as strict with G."

J. T.'s father was a Scotchman who deserted her mother after she had borne him two children, to "Go back home and be married," as J. told me. J. had been brought up in an orphan asylum until her twelfth year, when she had been placed by her mother in the family of a hair-dresser, masseuse and manicure, for whom she worked after school and to whom she was apprenticed. J.'s mother was a housemaid and spent her "afternoon off" with J. taking her to the park or to the "movies" but, and J. wept bitterly as she related it, "Mother is a church member and she won't let me go to Sunday School because she don't want people to know I belong to her."

T. M. was tenderly cared for by her father's wife, Mrs. M., although her mother was Mrs. M.'s niece.

Additional instances of irregular families were found in the cases of the exceptional children.

The above mentioned instances were not specially reported children; and the facts were gleaned in the regular course of house to house visiting. On the other hand, out of more than five hundred homes visited, less than twenty-five bore any visible stamp of irregularity; and since the information concerning irregular conditions was given quite frankly and freely, it is only fair to suppose that there was not a large percentage of concealment in regard to conditions in other families.

Without exception, in homes where there were step-mothers or fathers, the support of the children fell to the natural parent. Other household expenses were as a rule shared equally, but the mother or father as the case might be, supported the children, unless indeed, as happened in two instances, the children supported themselves. In the first of these, the mother stated that the child, a boy, was so frail that he would never be able to perform hard manual work, and she was anxious for him to secure an education so that he might be fitted for less arduous work. The mother herself was not working and there were no other children. The boy was working from four in the afternoon until twelve at night in the lavatory of a family hotel, where he had no fresh air and only artificial light. For this work he was receiving $12.00 a month!

In the other family there was a step-mother. The father was janitor of two steam-heated flat-houses for which he received the rent of a four-room apartment in the basement and $30.00 a month. All the work of attending to the garbage, scrubbing halls, etc., was performed by his children by his first wife.

In both these instances school records were suffering, and several visits had to be made in order to convince the parents that if home conditions were not remedied it would be necessary to appeal to the law or some social agency in behalf of the children.

With these two exceptions, however, the children were supported by their surviving parent.

The large number of men who were living away from home and not supporting their families constituted a noticeable hardship to the mothers. In not a single instance had the aid of the law been invoked to compel these men to provide for their children. Without exception the women gave as the reasons for not prosecuting their husbands or the fathers of their children, either their own lack of time to go to court, or a disinclination to force support from the delinquent man. When the whereabouts of the fathers were known, however, the custom was prevalent of sending the children to their father for money for their necessities. In two instances it was possible, where the father was away from the city, to get in touch with him through the Charity Organization Society and to secure from him at least temporary provision for his family.

II. School Children

The object of the study of colored school children, as stated in the chapter on Method and Scope of Investigation, was to learn what causes, if any, were active in affecting the school status of the children and their ability and opportunity to advance beyond the attainments of their parents and thus maintain their place in the march of events.

The preliminary survey indicated clearly that their social environment was affected by forces in which color or race consciousness played a more or less dominating rôle.

To what extent this fact is responsible for the school status of the children as disclosed by the intensive investigation, it is not possible to state with any degree of accuracy. It is fair to assume, however, that broken homes, illiterate parents, and the lack of care which is the result of the predominance of working mothers play their part in creating the conditions found. When to these causes is added the consciousness that schoolmates, teachers, and the community at large have to a greater or less extent a "color problem" in mind, the reaction of such consciousness must of necessity have its effect on the child.

The intensive study was begun January 1, 1913, and was carried on by the investigator during the following nine months in the schools and in the homes of the children.

The group studied includes 441 boys and girls in the public elementary schools, 37 girls in the Wadleigh High School and Annex, 15 boys in DeWitt Clinton High School, and 38 girls in the Manhattan Trade School, a total of 531. While the evening schools attended by colored pupils were also visited a number of times to secure information concerning tendency and opportunity, no intensive study of the pupils in them was attempted.

The information secured in this phase of the investigation will be considered under three heads: 1.—Elementary school pupils; 2.—High school pupils; and 3.—Manhattan Trade School pupils.

ELEMENTARY SCHOOL PUPILS

In selecting the 441 elementary school pupils whose records are compiled in this section, it was at first planned to consider only such children as had reached the grammar grades, that is, the fifth, sixth, seventh and eighth grades, as these children seemed to offer better material for noting ability and tendencies than those of the lower grades. For this purpose, the following colored children were studied: All in the 8th grades of P. S. 69 and P. S. 119, Manhattan; all in the 7th grades in P. S. 69; part of the 7th grade in P. S. 119, Manhattan; and all in the fifth and sixth grades in P. S. 100 and P. S. 141, Manhattan.

Later it was deemed advisable to study some children in the first grade, in order to learn the age at which children entered school under the most normal physical conditions, as well as the home conditions surrounding the beginning of their school career. For this purpose, the pupils in the Henrietta Day School of the Children's Aid Society were selected because the school is located in the heart of the San Juan Hill colored district. In addition, a group in P. S. 28, Manhattan, made up of children from families coming directly from the South or from families in which both parents were working or the children were not living with their parents was studied.

In connection with the study of exceptional children, it was also deemed advisable to study the entire group of truants and part of the pupils in ungraded classes in P. S. 89, Manhattan. These pupils were naturally not confined to the first, fifth, sixth, seventh or eighth grades as originally planned, but were scattered throughout the grades. This accounts for the fact that in the following tables a few pupils are found in some of the grades not originally contemplated in the study.

General School Conditions

In evaluating the material gathered from the schools studied, it was found that considerable allowance would have to be made because of the different ways in which the problems covered were approached and treated by principals and teachers in the various schools. This is particularly true of the problems of irregular attendance, and of the personal relations existing between the teachers and the colored pupils or their parents. In the larger schools, where, as a rule, the principals left the interviewing of parents to clerks, who could not be expected to bring as sound judgment to bear upon the situation as would the principal or head of department, there was naturally considerable misconception of general conditions and individual problems. The small school, in which the head of department was in charge of matters of attendance and discipline, did more efficient work and notification of absences and the remedying of tendencies toward truancy or misbehavior were in better control. In the case of the larger schools, however, parents frequently complained that there was much delay between the time of the child's absence and their receipt of information concerning it; and the children had the opportunity of becoming chronic truants before their parents or guardians had any information concerning their absence. In one school the following system of supervision of incipient truants was in force and showed excellent results. After an interview with parents or guardians an arrangement was made whereby the time of leaving home in the morning was noted by a responsible person in a book carried by the pupil, the teacher registering in the same book the time of reaching and of leaving school. The time of arrival at home, registered by the home authority, completed the record. Each week, the head of department checked up these books with teachers, pupils and home guardians. The plan was found to have a markedly good effect in disciplining the offenders.

Two schools were handicapped in dealing with the attendance problem by the fact that this was inextricably interwoven with other problems of the school. In one of them bad feeling between the boys and some of the teachers was so pronounced that it reached the public press on at least one occasion, when an indignant mother appeared in the school and physically chastised a man teacher for beating her son.

In special cases referred from this school there was a noticeable amount of tension between the teachers and pupils, and very little doubt that corporal punishment was used rather freely. The teachers admitted that they inflicted corporal punishment, but intimated that it would be impossible to exercise any sort of control without it. One of the teachers openly said that she felt that she was being degraded by teaching colored children, and the principal said that no response was received from the teachers to suggestions that parents' meetings be held. At the close of the investigation the principal was closely in touch with all the neighborhood agencies for colored people. At the request of one principal for help in furnishing a program for the Friday morning assemblies, he was placed in touch with the Music School Settlement for Colored People and since then many of his pupils have gone to the Settlement for lessons.

In another school personal antipathies played a prominent part, and problems of working parents plus these school antipathies between teachers and pupils created a situation that will require much smoothing over for some time to come. The school nurse was active in assisting with the social problems of this school, but far more time was required than she could give from her other duties to cope adequately with the situation. The school was not co-operating with any of the social agencies of the neighborhood. There were several complaints from clergymen that attempts to secure help in stopping crap games in front of the school house had met with rebuffs.

The attitude of the schools toward social activities also varied. Few of such activities existed. Branches of the Public Schools Athletic League, walking, swimming and folk dancing clubs, etc., were organized in four of the schools studied, i. e., P. S. 89, 100, 141 and 28. While the physical benefits derived from these activities is undoubted, they seem to have slight social significance, the atmosphere especially in the case of the Public Schools Athletic League being similar to that of the classroom.

One gratifying result of the investigation is the fact that a certain amount of misunderstanding by the school authorities of conditions among colored families was cleared up; as, for instance, the prevalent belief of school principals that colored men were idle and in a large percentage of cases supported by their wives. This belief was found to be based upon the fact that the fathers so often came to school in response to notes from the teacher and stated that the mothers had not come because they were at work. This custom was proven, by the intensive investigation, to be due in the large majority of cases to the fact that the father worked at night, part of the time, at any rate;

all elevator men in apartment houses, for instance, work in alternate night and day shifts.

In regard to the general complaint of difficulty in securing attention from colored parents to requests to call at the school, the investigation showed plainly that this was not due so much to neglect or indifference as to the fact that the parents complained of were, with few exceptions, working people, and the visit to school meant actual and hardly-to-be-sustained loss of money.

The effect of the unbiased consideration it was possible for a disinterested person to give to the adjustment of difficulties can hardly be over-estimated. Situations that were at high tension relaxed; and incipient enmities between pupil and teacher were smoothed over with little effort.

An instance of such adjustment is shown in the case of a boy, eight years of age, whose attendance was irregular and who was told on several occasions to ask his mother to come to the school. Notes to the parents brought no results. When this case was reported, the boy was recognized as belonging to a family whose father was a flagrant offender in keeping all his children out of school to perform his own tasks as janitor of a double apartment house, while he himself apparently did nothing but direct the work. The boy had been told by his teacher that he was being given a final warning and that he must bring his mother to school. He appeared the next morning without his mother; later he said that his teacher boxed his ears and he refused to go back to school. It was found on inquiry that the mother could not go to school on that occasion because she was in bed suffering with rheumatism of the feet, and that the father refused to go to see the teacher. The situation was explained to the teacher, and she not only understood it but said that she would visit the family and would try to use her influence with the father to be less exacting in the matter of home duties of the children.

Another instance was that of a girl of very high-strung, nervous temperament, who was reported as having insulted both her sewing teacher and her class teacher by unseemly mirth during the sewing lesson, and by throwing her sewing on the floor and generally "having a tantrum" when her class teacher rebuked her. She had been sent home and had refused to return. On visiting the home it was discovered that the girl was subject to severe nasal hemorrhages which were usually followed by fits of hysterical weeping. She had had a hemorrhage on the morning in question and had not wished to go to school; but her mother persuaded her to go and the customary hysteria followed. The girl was taken to a physician who found that she was suffering from a circulatory disturbance. She was placed under the care of a physician and the matter was explained to both teachers. The class teacher and the girl were afterwards the firmest possible friends, and the teacher declared that she was becoming more and more impressed with the forgiving nature of the colored girls.

The study brought to light other facts that applied to all the children, whether white or colored. It was found, for example, that systems of keeping records on pupils' cards varied widely as between the schools. In some schools, health records could not be secured because those records were made only on the set of cards in the possession of the teacher and were not transferred to the cards filed in the principal's office, the latter being the set used in the investigation. In other cases complete records were filed (see pp. 100–101).

Besides showing a varying attitude on the part of principals and teachers with regard to meeting and dealing with difficult conditions, the report discloses such a variety of ways in which the children were affected by these conditions that general conclusions are almost impossible. This is clearly illustrated by the following contrasted histories:

Two children, a boy and girl, among the youngest members of the normal group, the boy 9 years and 5 months, and the girl 9 years and 6 months old, while totally unrelated, even unacquainted, presented marked similarity in personality and temperament and the sharpest possible contrast in environment and opportunity. Both were bright, keen, eager, impulsive, attractive and responsive. The boy, neglected and in rags, was already busily engaged in assisting with the organization of a "gang" of street-boys after school. The girl, daintily clean, all perky bows and much given to delighted struttings on errands for "teacher," was her mother's closest chum. Both fathers were away from home. In the boy's case he was a waiter in a hotel at Garden City. The girl's father was a railroad conductor and came home only once a week. The boy's home was on the top floor of a tenement. His mother was a fretful, quarrelsome woman and was away from home at work all day. The boy ate a solitary breakfast, luncheon and, in the busy season, dinner, often preparing his own meals. The girl's mother said, "G. is all I have, and I must always be home when she is out of school." The boy's marks both for work and deportment were C and his teacher characterized his conduct as "troublesome" and his mentality as "fair." The girl had B for work and A for deportment. Her teacher called her "a lovely child" and stated that she was "very bright." One child was being given her chance in life; the other was growing up as the streets trained him. His older brother was in the Juvenile Asylum, committed for stealing.

Another group, this time two girls, in the same class of the same school, one 11 years and 5 months old, the other 11 years and 6 months old, also presented marked similarity of personality, tastes, manner and general personal equipment. Their circumstances were as different as those of the two children described above.

One, the fortunate one, was also the daughter of a railroad conductor. Her home was in a spacious apartment comfortably furnished. Her mother was occupied with her household and her children. The other was one of a brood of five, deserted by a drunken father. The mother went out to do cleaning every day in the week, and earned $1.50 a day, or $9.00 a week, on which she supported herself and five children. This marked difference in environment had, however, no apparent effect on the scholarship of these girls, and a study of the school records gave no hint as to the handicap under which one of them was working, for both were marked by their teachers B for work and B for conduct.

So contradictory have the results of the study often proved to be, therefore, that one would need to present in detail the individual problems connected with almost every one of the children visited, in order to present adequately the findings of the investigation.

School Status of Individual Children

The study of school records was made from cards on file in the principals' offices. The information gleaned included age, grade, mark for work, mark for conduct, and attendance. The marks for work and conduct were the average marks for the term ending with the Christmas holidays in 1912. In addition to the markings for work and for conduct, the teacher's estimate of the child's general capacity as regards mentality and character were secured. The number of years of school attendance in New York was also noted, where possible, and, in some cases, the attendance elsewhere. This latter information could not be considered accurate, as it was frequently found that data apparently covering all the school time in New York did not take into consideration the fact that pupils who had, at some previous time, attended school in New York, had gone to school elsewhere, and had been

TABLE II.—AGE GRADE TABLE OF NORMAL PUPILS (AGES AS OF SEPT. 1, 1912)

Grade	Age 5–6	6–6½	6½–7	7–7½	7½–8	8–8½	8½–9	9–9½	9½–10	10–10½	10½–11	11–11½	11½–12	12–12½	12½–13	13–13½	13½–14	14–14½	14½–15	15–15½	15½–16	16–16½	16½–17	17–17½	17½–18	18–18½	18½–19	Total	Under age	At age	Over age	Grade
1A....	16	12	2	4	5	..	..	1	..	..	..	..	..	..	..	..	..	..	..	..	..	..	..	..	..	..	..	40	16	14	10	1A
1B....	3	7	16	10	8	5	4	1	2	..	..	..	..	..	..	..	..	..	..	..	..	..	..	..	..	..	..	56	10	26	20	1B
2A....	..	..	..	..	..	..	..	..	..	..	..	..	..	..	..	..	..	..	..	..	..	..	..	..	..	..	..	..	..	..	..	2A
2B....	..	..	..	..	..	1	1	..	..	..	1	1	..	..	..	..	..	..	..	..	..	..	..	..	..	..	..	4	..	1	3	2B
3A....	..	..	..	..	..	..	..	..	1	1	..	..	..	..	..	..	..	..	..	..	..	..	..	..	..	..	..	2	..	..	2	3A
3B....	..	..	..	..	..	..	..	..	..	1	..	..	..	..	..	..	1	..	..	..	..	..	..	..	..	..	..	2	..	..	2	3B
4A....	..	..	..	..	..	..	..	..	1	..	..	..	..	..	..	..	..	..	..	..	..	..	..	..	..	..	..	1	..	1	..	4A
4B....	..	..	..	..	..	..	..	..	..	..	..	1	..	..	..	..	1	..	..	..	..	..	..	..	..	..	..	2	..	..	2	4B
5A....	..	..	..	..	..	1	..	..	2	4	6	7	7	7	5	1	3	1	2	..	..	..	..	..	..	..	..	46	3	10	33	5A
5B....	..	..	..	..	..	..	..	..	..	1	2	6	4	5	3	..	1	3	1	1	..	..	..	..	..	..	..	27	1	8	18	5B
6A....	..	..	..	..	..	..	..	..	..	..	1	2	2	5	3	1	2	2	1	1	..	..	..	..	..	..	..	20	1	4	15	6A
6B....	..	..	..	..	..	..	..	..	..	..	..	1	1	6	3	2	2	2	..	..	1	..	..	..	..	..	..	18	1	7	10	6B
7A....	..	..	..	..	..	..	..	..	..	..	..	..	..	..	2	1	2	3	3	2	1	..	1	..	..	..	..	15	..	2	13	7A
7B....	..	..	..	..	..	..	..	..	..	..	..	..	..	1	6	7	6	8	6	3	..	3	3	..	..	..	..	43	1	13	29	7B
8A....	..	..	..	..	..	..	..	..	..	..	..	..	..	..	..	2	5	4	6	4	3	7	2	..	..	..	1	34	..	7	27	8A
8B....	..	..	..	..	..	..	..	..	..	..	..	..	..	..	..	..	1	6	2	3	6	6	1	..	1	..	1	27	..	7	20	8B
Total	19	19	18	14	13	7	5	2	6	7	10	18	14	24	22	14	24	29	21	14	11	16	7	..	1	..	2	337	33	100	204	..

TABLE III.—AGE GRADE TABLE OF EXCEPTIONAL PUPILS (AGES AS OF SEPT. I, 1912)

NINETY-ONE PUPILS IN REGULAR CLASSES REPORTED FOR CAUSE

Grade	Over age	At age	Under age	Total	5–6	6–6½	6½–7	7–7½	7½–8	8–8½	8½–9	9–9½	9½–10	10–10½	10½–11	11–11½	11½–12	12–12½	12½–13	13–13½	13½–14	14–14½	14½–15	15–15½	15½–16	16–16½	16½–17	17–17½
1A	1	1	1	3	1	1			1																			
1B			1	1		1																						
2A	3	1		4				1			1					1	1											
2B	2			2								1	1															
3A	4	2	2	8				1	1	1	1	1		1			1	1										
3B	8	2		10							1	1	2				3	2		1								
4A	3			3													1	2										
4B	7	4		11									2	2	1	1		1	1	1		2						
5A	12	1	1	14								1			1	2	2	2	3		1		1	1				
5B	8	1		9											1		1		1	1	1		3		1			
6A	12			12														3	1	2	2	3		1		1		
6B	8	1		9													1		2		2	2						
7A	1			1																								1
7B	4			4																	1		3					
8A																												
8B																												
Total	73	13	5	91	1	2		2	2	1	3	4	5	3	3	4	10	11	8	5	7	7	8	2	1	1		1

92

entered later as new pupils on their return to the New York schools. Furthermore, owing to lack of official records, the period of attendance in schools outside of New York quoted in this report is frequently based merely on the memory of members of the family or of the child itself.

The 441 children considered in this section fall into two broad groups: the "normal" group, comprising 337 pupils, and the "exceptional" group, comprising 104 pupils. The age-grade distribution of the normal group is given in Table II, and the age-grade distribution of the "exceptional group" is given in Table III.

The group of exceptional children includes, in addition to 53 who were specially reported by principals and teachers, 40 truants who were studied because of the relation which their home conditions evidently bore to their school difficulties, and 11 ungraded class pupils. The age-grade distribution of this exceptional group, given in Table III, comprises only 91 out of the total of 104 children, as the 11 ungraded children mentioned above, together with 2 mentally defective children in the group of 53 above referred to, making a total of 13, could not be included in such a classification.

The grades in which the children are found in these two tables are the grades in which they were registered at the beginning of this investigation, January 1913, and the ages under which they are recorded are their ages of the preceding September, that is September 1, 1912, the approximate date of their beginning the work of these grades.

The most obvious fact revealed by both of these tables is the large proportion of over-age pupils. In the normal group, 60.5% are over-age for their grade, and, in the exceptional group, the retarded children aggregate 80.2% of the total number. As already pointed out in the preliminary survey, these pupils constituted the major problem of the colored child in the schools in which they were located. This fact is further emphasized when the extent of retardation in the several grades, as shown in Tables IV and V, is taken into consideration. It will be noted that the degree of retardation in the whole group ranges from less than one year to five years in both the normal and exceptional groups.

The at-age group in both the normal and exceptional groups (See Tables II and III) is relatively small and rather uniformly distributed through the grades.

94

TABLE IV.—NUMBER OF RETARDED CHILDREN, BY GRADE AND PERIOD OF RETARDATION—NORMAL GROUP

Grade	Less than ½	½, less than 1	1, less than 1½	1½, less than 2	2, less than 2½	2½, less than 3	3, less than 3½	3½, less than 4	4, less than 4½	4½, less than 5	Total
1A	4	5	..	..	1	..	..	..	..	..	10
1B	8	5	4	1	2	..	..	..	..	..	20
2B	1	..	..	..	1	1	..	..	..	..	3
3A	..	1	1	..	..	..	..	..	..	..	2
3B	..	1	..	..	..	..	..	..	1	..	2
4B	..	1	..	..	..	..	1	..	..	..	2
5A	7	7	7	5	1	3	1	2	..	..	33
5B	4	5	3	..	1	3	1	1	..	..	18
6A	5	3	1	2	2	1	1	..	..	..	15
6B	3	2	2	2	..	..	1	..	..	..	10
7A	1	2	3	3	2	1	..	1	..	..	13
7B	6	8	6	3	..	3	3	..	..	..	29
8A	4	6	4	3	7	2	..	..	..	1	27
8B	2	3	6	6	1	..	1	..	1	..	20
Total	45	49	37	25	18	14	9	4	2	1	204

TABLE V.—NUMBER OF RETARDED CHILDREN, BY GRADE AND PERIOD OF RETARDATION—EXCEPTIONAL GROUP

Grade	Less than ½	½, less than 1	1, less than 1½	1½, less than 2	2, less than 2½	2½, less than 3	3, less than 3½	3½, less than 4	4, less than 4½	4½, less than 5	Total
1A	..	1	..	..	..	..	..	..	..	..	1
2A	..	1	..	..	..	..	1	1	..	..	3
2B	..	1	1	..	..	..	..	..	..	..	2
3A	1	..	1	..	..	1	1	..	..	..	4
3B	2	..	..	..	3	2	..	1	..	..	8
4A	..	..	..	1	2	..	..	..	..	..	3
4B	1	1	..	1	1	1	..	2	..	..	7
5A	2	2	2	3	..	1	..	1	1	..	12
5B	1	..	1	1	1	..	3	..	1	..	8
6A	3	1	2	2	3	..	1	..	..	..	12
6B	2	..	2	2	..	..	..	1	..	1	8
7A	..	..	..	1	..	..	..	..	..	..	1
7B	1	..	3	..	..	..	..	..	..	..	4
Total	13	7	12	11	10	5	6	6	2	1	73

The under-age group of 33 in the normal group is made up almost exclusively of pupils in the 1A and 1B grades, who were under-age, for the most part, because they entered school before reaching the normal age. In all the other grades of this group combined only seven under-age pupils are found, which, in view of the large number of retarded children in the upper grades, would seem to indicate a strong tendency toward progressive retardation in the school life of the child. The exceptional group naturally shows a smaller percentage of under-age children than the normal group. In the latter case, the percentage is 9.8%, in the former only 5.5%. The total number, 5, is so small that less importance can be placed upon its distribution than upon the distribution of under-age children in the normal group. However, with one exception, it will be noted that all the 5 cases fall within the first three grades.

In Table II, giving the distribution as to grades and ages of children in the normal group, it was pointed out that 204, or 60.5%, of these children were retarded. An attempt was made to discover, if possible, through further study, some of the reasons for this great amount of retardation. Only 147 of these children could be found. Of the remaining 57, fifteen were not known at the address given on the school records except that in one case the janitor said the family in question had moved two years previously; eleven were said by janitors or neighbors to have moved out of town; eleven were called on three times without finding anyone at home, and twenty had moved and were not traced.

The records of the 147 children found showed first, that 98 had attended school in New York City only, and that 49 had attended school in New York and elsewhere. Secondly, 58, including 41 of those who had attended school in New York only and 17 of those who had attended school in New York and elsewhere, as shown in Table VI, had entered school over-age and had been in school the normal or less than the normal length of time required to make their grade. While these children were over-age for their grade and were therefore apparently retarded, they really constitute a rapid advancement group, although none of them were in E, or rapid advancement classes. Constituting, as they do, 28.4% of the total of 204 retarded children in the normal group, they tend to modify considerably the adverse conclusion that might be drawn from the statement already made that 60.5% of the normal group were retarded. It might truthfully be said that over one-fourth of the retarded children in the normal group were, in reality, artificially retarded, by reason of the fact that they had not been in school long enough to enable them to make their grade at a normal age. Only 89 of the 147 children in the so-called retarded group, therefore, constitute the truly retarded group, i. e., those children who, whether they entered school at, under or over age, had been in school longer than the normal time in which they should have made their grades.

TABLE VI.—PERIOD REQUIRED BY RETARDED PUPILS TO REACH GRADES

(A) PUPILS ATTENDING SCHOOL IN NEW YORK CITY ONLY

No. years less than normal time to reach grade	No. years over-age					Total
	Less than 1 year	1, less than 2 years	2, less than 3 years	3, less than 4 years	4, less than 5 years	
3 years or more...	..	..	..	..	..	..
2, less than 3 years.	..	..	1	..	..	1
1, less than 2 years.	5	3	2	..	..	10
Less than 1 year...	11	9	1	..	1	22
Normal time	5	3	..	..	..	8
Total..........	21	15	4	..	1	41

(B) PUPILS ATTENDING SCHOOL IN NEW YORK AND ELSEWHERE

No. years less than normal time to reach grade	No. years over-age					Total
	Less than 1 year	1, less than 2 years	2, less than 3 years	3, less than 4 years	4, less than 5 years	
3 years or more ...	..	..	..	..	..	..
2, less than 3 years.	..	..	..	..	..	..
1, less than 2 years.	2	2	..	..	..	4
Less than 1 year...	2	4	1	2	..	9
Normal time	..	1	1	2	..	4
Total..........	4	7	2	4	..	17

In the apparently retarded group of 58 children shown in Table VI, are some typical cases of children coming to New York from the South who had never been in school up to an advanced age:

W. H. B., 14 years old, in 3B grade, had been only two years in school, coming to New York from Virginia at the age of 12, with no previous schooling.

E. B., 12 years, 6 months old, in 5A grade, had been in school only 3 years, 4 months, coming to New York from Virginia.

L. S., 13 years, 10 months, in 5A grade, had been in school only 3 years, 4 months, although born in New York and living there all her life.

The 89 children in the truly retarded group can be subdivided as follows:

```
Attended New York schools and elsewhere:
    (a) Entered at or under age............    12
    (b) Entered over-age..................    20
                                             ——    32
Attended New York schools only:
    (a) Entered at or under age............    24
    (b) Entered over-age..................    33    57
                                                  ——
                                                  89
```

Of the 32 children in this group attending school in New York and elsewhere, only 3 were retarded because of non-promotion due to failure in their studies. Eleven had been demoted on coming to New York; 8 had been out of school for a term or longer because of illness; 4 had had an abnormal amount of absence because of poverty or illness in their homes, and 4 had been kept home to care for younger children.

One of the most aggravated cases was that of R. J., who had attended schools for colored children in Washington and Baltimore, graduating from the colored high school in the latter place, and who, on coming to New York at the age of 16, had been demoted to 7B in the elementary schools.

Another girl, who was graduated from high school at 18, had spent 8 years in the Alabama schools for colored people, where the schools are open only 7 months in the year and attendance is rendered irregular by the necessity for helping with farm work.

Of the 57 children attending school in New York only, 12

were in grades 1A and 1B and their over-age was due in each case to the incidental absences due to infantile diseases, such as mumps, measles, whooping cough, etc. Of the remaining 45, 14 were retarded because of non-promotion due to failure in their studies. All of these pupils were marked C for work. Ten were absent for one or more terms because of illness; 11 had been irregular in attendance at one time or another because of illness or poverty at home, and 10 had been absent frequently to care for younger children.

The list of localities from which colored children in this retarded group came to New York comprises the following:

Norfolk, Va.	1	Long Branch, N. J.	2
Bermuda	2	Jamaica, B. W. I.	2
Philadelphia	4	Jacksonville, Fla.	1
Trinidad, W. I.	1	Porto Rico	1
Danish W. I.	1	Hamilton, B. W. I.	1
Boston	2	British Guiana	1
St. Thomas, W. I.	1	Darlington, S. C.	1
Georgia (county school)	1	Kent Island, Me.	1
Barbados	34	Portland, Me.	1
Henderson, N. C.	1	St. Croix, Danish W. I.	1
Putnam, Conn.	1	Baltimore, Md.	1
Charleston, S. C.	3	Birmingham, Ala.	1
Alexandria, Va.	1	Charlotte, N. C.	1
Cumberland, Va.	1	Antigua, W. I.	1
Riverdale, N. Y. (Orphan Asylum)	2	Paris, France	1
Savannah, Ga.	2	Dobbs Ferry, N. Y.	1
Washington, D. C.	2	Asbury Park, N. J.	1
Baltimore, Md.	2	Atlanta, Ga.	1

A digest of the marks for work and conduct (Table VII) shows a decided tendency to the average or B grade of child for work, with a somewhat higher rating for conduct. The exceptional group naturally shows a smaller percentage of high grade children. The average or B grade children number about the same in this as in the normal group; but the percentage of low-grade (C and D) children is much higher than in the normal group.

In examining the subjects in which the children were deficient, arithmetic appeared to be the *bête noire* of all groups. In discussing one pupil's deficiency in this subject with her mother, she said they had tried every available means of overcoming the child's difficulty and had finally decided that the newspapers (it was at the time comment on the school inquiry of the Board of Estimate and Apportionment was being published) were right in saying that arithmetic was not taught properly in the schools. General deficiency occurred to the largest extent among the exceptional children, as was to be expected.

TABLE VII.—NUMBER AND PER CENT OF CHILDREN IN NORMAL AND EXCEPTIONAL GROUPS HAVING DESIGNATED MARKS IN WORK AND CONDUCT

Group	Total number of children	Work						Conduct					
		A		B		C and D		A		B		C and D	
		No.	Per cent.	No.	Per cent.	No.	Per cent.	No.	Per cent.	No.	Per cent.	No.	Per cent.
Normal													
Under-age......	33	12	36.4	14	42.4	7	21.2	18	54.6	9	27.3	6	18.1
At-age.........	100	22	22.0	63	63.0	15	15.0	49	50.0	40	40.0	11	10.0
Over-age.......	204	30	14.7	127	62.2	47	23.1	94	46.1	95	46.5	15	7.4
Total—normal.	337	64	18.9	204	57.5	69	23.6	161	47.6	144	42.6	32	9.8
Exceptional....	90*	3	4.4	48	52.7	39	42.9	18	19.7	48	52.7	25	27.6

* One child, a tuberculous cripple, died during the investigation, reducing the total of 91, as given in Table III, to 90.

A study of attendance shows little variability as between the under-age, at age, and over-age of the normal group, the at-age group somewhat curiously having the lowest percentage. The attendance of these groups was as follows:

```
Under-age group ( 33 children) attendance average.... 91.3%
At-age     group (100    "    )      "        "    .... 89.5%
Over-age    "    (204    "    )      "        "    .... 92.2%
Average for total Normal Group (337 children)........ 91.3%
   "     "  Exceptional    "    (89*    "    )........ 78.3%
   "     "  total of 426 children.................... 88.3%
```

The general average for the normal group, 91.3 per cent., is good; in fact, it is better than the average attendance for the entire city, which is 89 per cent.† The exceptional group, however, shows a considerably lower general average, 78.3 per cent., which would be somewhat lower if it were not raised by two pupils marked "A" for work whose attendance in both cases was over 90 per cent. The average attendance for all the children studied, 88.3 per cent., differing as it does by only 0.7 of 1 per cent. from the general average of 89 per cent. for the entire city, bears out only to a very slight extent the contention of the school authorities, as stated in the preliminary survey, that poor attendance next to over-age constitutes the most acute problem of the colored school child. It is probably more nearly correct to say that it constitutes one of the most acute problems of the entire school population.

In both normal and exceptional groups attendance, like charity, was found to cloak many ills, and what appeared in the school record as merely an absence meant anything from a passing indisposition to the gravest misfortune or delinquency.

It would have been extremely interesting to make some deductions regarding health and its influence on scholarship and attendance, but the health records were too incomplete on the cards studied to offer much of value or significance. It was not possible to work in the classrooms, and neither during the noon hour nor after school was it feasible to have access to the class cards for a sufficient period of time to select the cards of colored

---

* Two children in the group of 91 exceptional children did not have attendance marks, as these children were tuberculous and had been out of school for some time. They were reported for the purpose of having them placed in sanatoria.

† Report of City Superintendent of Schools for year ending July 31, 1913, Table II.

students for the purpose of securing health records. There are, therefore, wide gaps in these records and not much of value may be gleaned from the number secured. It was found, however, in several instances that children who had attended the same schools from kindergarten to the sixth and seventh grades had no health records noted on their cards; and these children said they had never been examined by a school physician.

Of the normal group of 337 children, only 167 cards with health records noted on them were found. Some of these children had only one physical defect; many had several. Among the more prevalent and important defects were the following: defective teeth, 74; defective vision, 12; defective breathing or tonsils, or both, 36; weak throats, 1; heart weakness, 2. Fifty-eight were stated to be in normal health. Of 91 in the exceptional group, 41 had no physical record on their cards. Of the remaining 50: 10 had defective teeth; 3, defective vision; 7, defective breathing or tonsils, or both; 3, tuberculosis; and 6, various troubles. Twenty-one were stated to be in normal health. It is hard to believe that so large a proportion of this "difficult" group was physically normal.

Teachers, with one or two exceptions, paid little attention to health in relation to the standing of pupils, and much misconception of certain situations could not fail to arise in consequence. Pupils recently convalescent from scarlet fever, pneumonia, etc., were characterized as lazy and unambitious, and a child who returned to school after a two years' absence because of spinal meningitis was reported stupid and inattentive. The disabilities were clearly the result of disease, the children's previous records bearing no relation to the faults mentioned.

Malnutrition was one of the most serious conditions that could be studied in this connection. Only 15 cases were noted on the cards; of these, out of eleven visited, only three (numbers 7, 10 and 11 below), could be traced directly to poverty:

Under-age Normal Group
1. D. M., 11 years 5 months old; 6B grade; lived in 4-room flat with mother and father and two younger children; income, $14.00; mother not working. Mother said that D. was in such a hurry in the morning and at noon that she never ate enough. D. had defective teeth and hypertrophied tonsils.
2. A. C., 10 years 6 months old; 5B grade; lived with aunt who stayed at home; father died in child's infancy and

mother was a housemaid; very good home; 4 rooms with uncle and aunt and three small children. Aunt said (and A. confirmed statement) that A. had everything she wished for in the way of food. A. had defective teeth, defective vision and hypertrophied tonsils.

3. E. C., 10 years old; 5A grade; lived with mother and two older children in 3 rooms; father dead; family income, $10.00 a week; evidently no lack of food. E. had defective teeth.

At-age Normal Group

4. F. H., 12 years 4 months old; lived with mother and father and 4 younger children in 3 rooms; family income, $18.00 a week; had little recreation; father very strict; apparently no lack of food, but living conditions bad; one brother delinquent; no other physical defects.

Over-age Normal Group

5. D. E., 13 years 4 months old; 6B grade; aunt and cousin, in 3 rooms; aunt cooked in day nursery; cousin suffered from venereal disease; D. said she often ate her meals standing in order to get back to school in time; did not like breakfast: no other physical defects; mother and father both dead.

6. R. B., 13 years 4 months old; 6B grade; lived with mother, four lodgers and younger sister in 6 rooms; family income about $12.00 a week; father living in Bermuda; mother said R. ate too hastily because of hurry to get to school; prepared breakfast and fed younger children at lunch; roller skates after school; no other physical defects.

7. M. H., 12 years 7 months old; 5B grade; lived with grandmother and 2 younger children on $5.00 a week; father and mother dead; physical defects.

8. A. E., 12 years old; 5A grade; lived with mother, 2 brothers and aunt in 3 rooms; income about $4.00 per week; father not living; hypertrophied tonsils; aunt helped some with expenses.

9. M. A., 10 years 3 months old; 3A grade; lived with mother, father, sister and brother in six rooms; not allowed out of doors after school; family income about $20.00 a week; subject to colds; no other physical defects.

Exceptional Group

10. W. S., 12 years 7 months old; 6A grade; lived with mother, 2 younger and 1 older child in four rooms; father dead; family income, $7-8 a week; defective teeth; often kept out of school to care for younger children, also because mother had no money to buy clothing for school.

11. A. S., 12 years 6 months old; 3A grade; lived with mother and 2 younger children in mission home; mother de-

serted; youngest child one month old; mother and sister scrubbed floor at mission. (Since close of investigation has become T. B.)

The remaining four children could not be found. On the other hand, malnutrition was discovered among a number of children other than the fifteen above referred to, whose school records contained no mention of it. For example:

M. K. and her four sisters and brother were supported by their mother on $9.60 a week, $5.00 of which was paid for rent. These children were examined at a dispensary and were found in an advanced stage of under-nourishment, their abdomens being distended from chronic slow starvation.

L. Q. was placed successively with four uncles and aunts by an immoral mother, and was found to be emaciated, irritable and of slow mentality.

J. E. and his brother, deserted by father and mother, were being cared for by their grandmother, who also supported her mother by day's work and washing. She said, "When we don't have anything else to eat, we eat bread, but we all share alike." The boys' conduct was troublesome and their mark for work was "C." They were thin to emaciation, and the older boy, 10 years, 5 months old, was eager to be out of school and at work.

C. M., marked B. for work and conduct, an illegitimate boy, living with his mother and grandmother both of whom worked, was thin and listless, although the family income was $10.00–$12.00 a week and there was an ample supply of food. C. said, "Sometimes I forget to eat my breakfast and lunch."

These instances emphasize the necessity already pointed out for close contact between home and school, in order that the child's problem may be intelligently studied and solved.

Status of Home Life

The statement by the school authorities that broken homes and working mothers were largely responsible for poor attendance and scholarship among colored children is borne out by the intensive investigation. In Table VIII, dealing with these questions, the families of only 248 children in the normal group and 86 in the exceptional could be considered, as facts could be secured only for this number.

Reference to Table VIII shows that, in the normal group, only 40.8% of the children, and, in the exceptional group, a still smaller number, 23.2%, were found living with both their parents. There was a larger number of step-fathers and step-mothers in the homes of the exceptional children than in the normal group—11.6% as against 8%. The number of children living with their mothers only, the father being either dead or away from home, was also larger in the exceptional than in the normal group—42% as against 33.4%. Only a small per cent. in either group was found living with their fathers only, the mothers being dead or away from home. These children made up 4% of the normal and 5.8% of the exceptional group. Thirteen per cent of the children of the normal group and 15.1% of the exceptional group were living with other relatives, while a mere handful, .8% of the normal and 2.3% of the exceptional group lived apart from relatives.

TABLE VIII.—NUMBER AND PER CENT OF CHILDREN LIVING WITH PARENTS OR OTHER PERSONS

Person or persons with whom child was living	Normal group		Exceptional group	
	No.	Per cent.	No.	Per cent.
Both parents..................	101	40.8	20	23.2
Both parents (stepfather or step-mother)......................	20	8.0	10	11.6
Mother only....................	83	33.4	36	42.0
Father only....................	10	4.0	5	5.8
Other relatives.................	32	13.0	13	15.1
Apart from relatives............	2	.8	2	2.3
Total......................	248	100.0	86	100.0

A curious family arrangement was found in the case of one of the children of the exceptional group. A boy, E. S., 9 years, 9 months old, in the 4B grade, was kept out of school because he had no shoes. On visiting the home address given in the school it was found that he and his sister were being given their meals there by their father's wife, but slept in the home of their mother who was never married and who had had two other children by other fathers. The father was in the West, employed in a large hotel, and had sent no money for the maintenance of the boy and his sister for six weeks. Mrs. S. was very ill with what proved later to be pernicious anæmia, and could not earn enough money to care for the children. After much persuasion she permitted the matter to be placed in the hands of the Charity

Organization Society, whose efforts brought a substantial response from her husband. She refused, however, to permit
application to be made for the commitment of the children. She
was a refined, intelligent woman, a West Indian of French descent,
and said she wished the children to be in their mother's custody
if she herself was no longer well enough to care for them. When
asked whether she thought it was doing justice to the children
to have them brought up by a woman of loose morals, she said,
"I should not regard Miss H. (their mother) as a woman of loose
morals. She is and always has been a very hardworking young
woman, and if I make myself content with these arrangements,
I cannot see why the public should feel concerned."

One little chap, 9 years 11 months old, in the 2B grade, was,
on the other hand, apparently suffering from the sins of a re-
calcitrant mother who had "run away with another man," as
his father said. The father had divorced her and married again.
The second wife was so completely devoted to her husband that
because he worked at night as a chauffeur she also secured night
employment that she might be at home with him during the
day. The boy was evidently in the way, and was given money
to buy his lunch outside and was not permitted to come home
till supper time after his parents had gone to work, leaving his
meal prepared for him. The boy expressed himself with great
difficulty, and it was apparent that he had little opportunity to
talk with anyone. This case was one referred to a philanthropic
agency with full data, but nothing was done and the boy later
developed into a chronic truant.

Another child, an orphan, well cared for in a comfortable
home, had no companionship except that of a bed-ridden grandmother who refused to permit her to associate with other girls
"because they were so bad." In consequence, the child's whole
life revolved around school and making fancy work at her grandmother's bedside. The grandfather and the uncle were longshoremen and were absent all day and most of the night.

A pertinent question regarding these broken families was
whether one or both of the parents were dead or were not living
at home. Only 147, or 59.2%, out of this total of 248 children
in the normal group had both parents living; and in a still
smaller percentage of families, 101, or 40.7%, were both father
and mother living at home. The exceptional group showed 39
children, or 45.3%, both of whose parents were living; and only
20, or 23.2%, both of whose parents were living at home.

TABLE IX.—WORKING MOTHERS

Group	Total number of children	Mother at home							Mother away from home							
		Not working — Father working		Working — Father working		Working — Father dead or away		Total		Working — Father working		Father not working		Father dead or away		Total	
		No.	Per cent.	No.	Per cent.	No.	Per cent.	No.	Per cent.	No.	Per cent.	No.	Per cent.	No.	Per cent.	No.	Per cent.
Normal																	
Under-age......	19	4	21.0	1	5.3	1	5.3	6	31.6	6	31.6	..	..	7	36.8	13	68.4
At-age........	76	22	28.9	12	15.9	3	3.9	37	48.7	23	30.3	2	2.6	14	18.4	39	51.3
Over-age......	143	30	21.0	24	16.8	8	5.6	62	43.4	32	22.3	3	2.1	46	32.2	81	56.6
Total—normal	238	56	23.5	37	15.6	12	5.0	105	44.1	61	25.6	5	2.1	67	28.2	133	55.9
Exceptional ..	66	1	1.5	12	18.2	3	4.5	16	24.2	22	33.3	..	..	28	42.5	50	75.8

Second only to the question of broken families is that of the working mother, as shown in Table IX. The total comprising this table is less than that in the groups considered in Table VIII, because it was impossible in many cases to secure the reasons for the parents' absence from home. Facts could be obtained from 238 families only in the normal group and 66 in the exceptional.

In the normal group, 105 mothers (44.1%) were at home and 133 (55.9%) were away from home, working. Of the mothers at home 56 were not working and 37 were working, and in both cases the fathers were living at home and supporting or partially supporting the family. The remaining 12 were either widows or deserted. Of the group of 133, 61 were partly supported by their husbands, 67 were either widows or deserted and 5 were apparently supporting their husbands at home. Of the entire normal group, therefore, only 56 mothers (23.5%) were at home, not working, the father supporting the family.

Of the exceptional group, in only 16, or 24.2%, out of 66 families were the mothers at home, while in 50 families, or 75.8%, the mothers were away from home at work. Of the first group one was not working, twelve were working in homes which the father also supported, and three were working at home as the sole support of the family. In the second group of 50, 22 mothers were partly supported by their husbands, the remaining 28 being widowed or deserted.

It is very evident from this table how much larger a proportion of the mothers of the normal children were at home where they could watch closely over the welfare of their children. In the cases of those children who had been reported by principals and teachers as in difficulty for one reason or another, (exceptional group), only 24.2% had mothers who were at home throughout the day, while in the normal group as high a per cent as 44.1 were living under these more favorable conditions.

Even more striking is the contrast between the normal and exceptional groups in cases where the mother was living at home and not working, thus being able to devote all of her time to the care of her home and children. In the normal group there were 56, or 23.5% so situated, small enough at best, while in the exceptional group there was only one, or 1.5%.

The frequency with which widowed or deserted mothers were found in the exceptional group as a whole as compared with the normal group as a whole, while not so striking, is, nevertheless, significant. In the former case there were 31 (3 at home and 28 away from home) or 47.0% of the total so situated, and in the latter case 89 (12 at home and 67 away from home) or 37.4% of the total.

In both groups, as previously stated, economic necessity predominated as the reason for the mother's absence from home; but in a number of instances, the desire for an outside interest or a veritable fury of industry on the part of the whole family left the children without after-school guidance of any sort.

After-school Activities

In studying the after-school activities of the various groups of colored children, it was possible to complete the records in 314 cases. The small under-age group was omitted because it comprised so many of the younger children of whom nothing very characteristic could be learned. The remaining 94 children which make up the original group of 441, had either moved away when the study of their out of school work and recreation was made or so little could be learned of their lives that they were not included in the number studied for after-school activities. The 314 children studied are grouped as follows:

```
At age...................................................  80
Over-age...............................................153
Exceptional ..........................................  81
```

All the activities, both work and play, which were discovered fall under the following heads:

Home work, including housework, errands, jobs not errands, care of children.
Sunday School.
Street Play.
Home Play.
School clubs (P. S. A. L., etc.).
Settlement or Church clubs.
Visiting.
Entertainments, socials, etc.
Theatre.
"Movies."
Basket-ball.
Lodge club.
Music lesson.
Boy Scouts.
Camp Fire Girls.
Home studying.

In summing up, all clubs have been considered together but the lodge clubs actually appear in only three instances. Most of the children have more than one activity, as appears in the tables.

TABLE X.—TABLE SHOWING COMPARATIVE FREQUENCY OF
DIFFERENT FORMS OF HOME-WORK

	At-age group (80 children)	Over-age group (153 children)	Exceptional group (81 children)	Total (314 children)
Housework........	29	73	29	131
Errands..........	5	26	27	58
Jobs not errands...	9	15	11	35
Care of children....	3	14	5	22

A surprising number of children in all the groups were busy at home and this
did not mean in any case in the manufacture of commercial articles. Several
boys earned money, however by helping the janitor, selling newspapers, washing dishes and doing errands. Carrying home laundry, sweeping, mending and
washing clothes are some of the duties under "housework" and "jobs other
than errands." Nine girls were making or helping to make their own clothes
and several others sewed at home or with dressmakers.

Many children in the at-age group had no form of homework on account of
their age, 29 of the 80 being under eight years of age. Of the exceptional
group twenty had at some time been sent to correctional institutions or had
become confirmed truants.

TABLE XI.—TABLE SHOWING COMPARATIVE FREQUENCY OF
AFTER-SCHOOL RECREATION

	At-age group (80 children)	Over-age group (153 children)	Exceptional group (81 children)	Total (314 children)
Sunday School.....	72	133	30	235
Clubs............	16	43	10	69
"Movies"........	20	42	16	78
Street play........	28	36	40	104
Home play........	14	17	12	41
Visiting..........	18	35	3	56
Entertainments	9	31	9	49
Theatre..........	11	17	6	34
Home study.......	7	27	4	38
Music lessons......	10	20	3	33
Basket-ball........	1	4	..	5
Boy Scouts........	..	..	6	6
Camp Fire Girls...	..	3	..	3

Some children in the at-age group had as many as six forms of
activity. All had at least two.

In the exceptional group, out of 15 forms of activity including
homework, 9 children had one activity; 19 children had two

activities; 26 children had three activities; 20 children had four activities; 7 children had five activities.

As no child in this group had more than five forms of activity and as all but twenty were busy with some sort of home work, and as street play and the "movies" were the most popular forms of recreation, the inference is easy. Sunday School cannot be classed as a form of recreation nor does it often connect itself with activities throughout the week. Its existence, however, cannot but be valuable.

Of 13 children in ungraded classes and included in this group, all were busy at home. One boy sold papers, seven did errands, two boys helped with the janitor's work. All attended Sunday School and eight went frequently to the "Movies." Two were Boy Scouts and one boy belonged to a settlement club. This record would be hard to duplicate in any similar group of children of another race.

The most salient feature in the tables is an almost unbroken column of Sunday School attendance. Of 314 children, only 79 failed to attend Sunday School regularly. On the other hand, the activity showing the lowest number is the Camp Fire Girls, there being only three. Five of the normal children played basketball and there were six Boy Scouts, all in the exceptional group.

The children having no home duties were almost invariably too young to be so occupied, although in a few instances studying in the final school year made attention to home duties impossible.

The very young children, those in grades 1A and 1B, were for the most part limited to Sunday School, street and home play. Those over ten years old, however, had home duties, varying from running errands to the entire care of the house, in half a dozen instances even including the making of the child's own clothes.

"Movies," it goes without saying, were popular with the majority of the children. Visiting and entertainments—which meant usually church entertainments—were next in popularity.

Only fourteen belonged to the Public Schools Athletic League and thirty-two to settlement, church or lodge clubs. Thirty-eight were engaged in home study.

As stated previously, no attempt was made by any of the parents or the social agencies visited to correlate outside activities with the children's school needs.

Girls in the 8A and 8B classes found themselves too much occupied with their studies, as a rule, to have any other interests but in the other grades little if any account was taken of the child's school progress in measuring his capacity for outside activities. The street play, viewed in its entirety, seems unusually healthful and zestful in the colored neighborhoods. Roller-skating, base-ball, the precarious "roller-skate automobiles," made of two tandem rollers with packing box strips mounted for a foot-board, are everywhere. "London Bridge" flourishes among groups of little girls. Housekeeping establishments on the front steps of flats are not allowed by janitors but nevertheless are ubiquitous. But back of it all is the feeling that few watchful eyes are guarding against accidents, and that day after day these street children are forming their habits and thoughts from the flotsam and jetsam of the street life that is the only life they have.

2. HIGH SCHOOL PUPILS

The fact that at the time the investigation was made only 15 colored boys were registered in De Witt Clinton High School, and only 36 girls in Wadleigh High School and Annex, is no measure, it was learned from talks with numbers of colored men of affairs, of the extent to which colored boys and girls are receiving more than a common school education.

Colored people of means, as a rule, send their sons and daughters to standard colleges and preparatory schools conducted exclusively for colored people. Clergymen, publicists and professional men who had sent their sons and daughters away to school, stated that there were so many social attractions in New York for young people it was well-nigh impossible to keep them interested in their studies.

It may therefore be assumed that, among the high school boys in particular, the pupils are not fairly representative either in number or calibre of the element in the colored population that is seeking to man the professions and other occupations requiring so-called higher education.

The principal of the boys' high school felt that the colored boys in that school were not promising. He was, indeed, doubtful if the high school curriculum could in the future be maintained at anything like its present standard because of the increasingly inferior calibre of all the pupils, of whatever nationality, which he attributed to our inability to assimilate our immigrant population fast enough for educational purposes. He felt, however, that even though their poorest Latin pupil was an Italian, and the most hopeless student of German was a Jew, the colored boys were even further removed, in their mental equipment, from the material that gave promise of benefitting them to any great extent from high school training.

The mentality estimate by teachers as given in Table XII showed only 9 of the 15 pupils to be of average or better than average calibre, considering 60 as an average.

TABLE XII.—CLASS AVERAGE AND ESTIMATED MENTALITY OF 15 DeWITT CLINTON HIGH SCHOOL BOYS

No.	Mentality	Marking
1	Good....................................	61
2	Below average............................	57
3	Low....................................	28
4	Above average...........................	61
5	Below average............................	65
6	Fair....................................	62
7	Better than average.......................	77
8	Normal.................................	59
9	Not up to average........................	58
10	Not high...............................	45
11	Poor...................................	48
12	Average................................	75
13	Good..................................	64
14	Fair...................................	75
15	Rather good............................	70

The record of the girls of the high school studied shows a higher grading. Fifteen out of the 37 received a rating of "satisfactory" as to mentality. The principal was more optimistic than the principal of the boys' school, and said that the colored girls who came to him presented quite as many grades of intelligence and character as did the white girls. He agreed with the elementary school principals' statements that the calibre of the girls was closely related to the quality of the home life to which they were accustomed.

Both the teachers and the pupils felt that the lack of any help at home in their high school work was a serious handicap. The girls were especially prone to fall into despair at their failure to grasp the first year's work in algebra and Latin; and eight girls had made up their minds either to leave school or to change from an academic to a technical course, in spite of their parents' willingness and ability to have them complete their education. They had evidently given little thought to what the completion of their education would mean to them as individuals; but, after receiving advice, they apparently saw the advisability of going on, even though the struggle was almost a cruel one.

As suggested in another part of the report, the need for tutoring among these boys and girls seems to be vital, and it is to be hoped that those interested in stimulating intellectual ambition in the race will place both teachers and pupils in touch with facilities for securing such service, especially during vacation periods.

The list of occupations of 16 mothers and 19 fathers of high school boys and girls speaks for itself in showing how little aid or stimulus is available at home:

Occupation of Fathers		*Occupation of Mothers*	
Porters..................	3	Laundresses...............	4
Waiters.................	3	Housemaids...............	3
Chefs....................	2	Janitress.................	1
Pullman porter...........	1	Dressmaker seamstresses.....	3
Moving van business........	2	Caretaker.................	1
Barber...................	1	Day's work...............	2
Watchman................	1	Operator on lace curtains.....	1
Elevator man.............	1	Maid in dry goods store......	1
Assistant janitor...........	1		
Attendant in animal hospital..	1	Total...................	16
Ministers.................	3		
Total..................	19		

Three of the high school girls visited expected to teach in the South after completing their high school course, as the standards in many of these states do not demand normal school training. The remaining number of girls expected to become teachers in New York. One or two had plans, not definitely formulated, however, of becoming trained nurses. All the girls visited were told about the need for social service among their own people. Without exception they were all interested in those church societies for young people whose activities were of a purely social or religious character; they also expressed much interest in educational activities of which they were told, and seemed anxious to be placed in touch with avenues through which they might learn to direct their own efforts.

The boys seemed to have no definite ambitions or plans, except in two instances. In one of these, the "boy" was a man of 37, who had come to New York from British Guiana where he had been teaching school. He was employed as an elevator man in an apartment house, attending school as his hours permitted, and was preparing himself for the ministry. In the other instance, the

9

"boy" was 21 years old and was a switchboard operator in an apartment house. He wished to study medicine later, if he could devise ways and means for doing so. Ten of the boys were employed after school and their occupations were as follows:

Order boys, grocery company	2
Errand boys	2
Porter	1
Messenger in hotel (bell-boy)	1
Program boy in theatre	1
General work, florist's shop	1
Elevator man in apartment house	1
Switchboard operator in apartment house	1

None of the girls had any occupation other than helping their mothers with home duties; and most of them said their studies were so difficult that they had very little time even for that.

The fact that the boys were engaged for a number of hours in gainful pursuits, while the girls had only their studies to occupy their time out of school, may account for the higher standard of scholarship among the girls.

The girls devoted their Saturdays to attending theatre, playing tennis, basket ball, attending meetings of Camp Fire Girls, etc., while, with only three exceptions, the boys worked all day.

The number of both boys and girls attending high school in New York city at the time of the investigation was infinitesimal, but is no indication of the educational progress of New York Negroes of the coming generation, as there is no means of knowing how many are attending the many high schools for Negro boys and girls that are maintained in the South, as well as in Pennsylvania and New Jersey and those now coming into existence in New York State, as, for instance, the agricultural college at Binghamton, etc.

3. MANHATTAN TRADE SCHOOL PUPILS

The 38 girls whose records in the Manhattan Trade School were studied include 15 girls who had graduated in previous years and 23 who were students there at the time of the investigation. This last group had been admitted for the year 1912–13, all of them to the dressmaking department.

As stated in another part of the report, the principal of the school found it difficult, if not impossible, to place colored girls in any other field of work, although she and her placement secretary said they had made no effort to discover a field of work for these girls among their own race. She also said she was obliged, because of the difficulty in placing the colored girls, to require a higher standard of qualification for admitting them to the trade school; and even given the desired qualifications, she questioned the advisability of admitting anything like a large proportion of colored pupils, because of the probable effect this might have in the attendance of white pupils.

That the qualifications secured were high is shown by the fact that of the 23 girls entered as pupils, four had attended high schools for a year or more, fourteen had been graduated from elementary school, one had completed 8A, one 7A, one 7B, while one had left school in grade 6A and one in 6B respectively.

An examination of the records of fifteen colored girls who had been graduated from the Manhattan Trade School in previous years, as shown in Table XIII, developed the fact that in the majority of cases the progress made by the girls was slow but hopeful; also that race prejudice was encountered among both employers and fellow workers.

TABLE XIII.—EMPLOYMENT RECORDS OF FIFTEEN COLORED GIRLS FROM THE MANHATTAN TRADE SCHOOL

Occupation	Number of positions held since leaving school	First pay	Last pay noted
Assistant finisher (record covers two months)	5	$5.00	Not given
Shopper and errands	5	4.00	$8
Finisher	6	4.00	5–6
Assistant finisher, later machine operator	9	4.00	7
Assistant finisher and hemstitcher	3	5.00	9
Embroidery; finisher	5	6.00	7
Skirt hand	3	5.00	7
Assistant finisher; skirts	5	5.00	6
Assistant finisher	4	5.00	6.50
Assistant finisher	4	5.00	4
Assistant finisher	4	5.00	5
Assistant finisher	3	5.00	5
Waist finisher	2	5.00	10
Assistant on skirts	6	5.00	6
Not given	—	—	—

Employers' reports show varying degrees of approval:

"Not satisfactory." No reason given.

"Laid off because of seasonal work; not satisfactory."

"Very satisfactory to employers."

"Slow at first, but improved."

"Satisfactory to employer."

"Went into private dressmaking work. Doing well."

"Unfortunate. Ill and not satisfactory."

"Knows nothing except sewing on hooks and eyes."

"Objection because of color."

"Satisfactory. In line for promotion."

"Liked by employer."

One employer stated to the school that a girl was called up on the telephone by white men. When asked how it was known that the men were white, the school secretary said she did not know; but the record of this remark was placed on the girl's card, nevertheless.

The list of occupations of parents given below shows that the girls were fitting themselves at any rate to keep pace with the status of their parents, if not, indeed, to progress beyond it.

Occupation of Fathers		*Occupation of Mothers*	
Baker	1	Seamstress	1
Coachman	1	Laundresses	11
Cooks	2	Dressmakers	4
Waiter	1	Janitor	1
Expressman	1	Housekeeper	1
Messengers	2	Waitress	1
Porters	2	Maid	1
Elevator man	1	None (supported by husband)	11
Longshoremen	2	Dead, or not living at home	2
Street cleaner	1	Not given	5
Clerks	2		
Furnaceman	1	Total	38
Chauffeur	1		
Carpenters	2		
Bricklayer	1		
Sexton	1		
Dead, or not living at home	13		
Not given	3		
Total	38		

In visiting pupils in the 7th and 8th grades of P. S. 119, fifteen said they were on the waiting list of the Manhattan Trade School but had not yet been admitted.

In talking with the mothers of these girls, the advisability of having the girls placed as apprentices with colored dressmakers or milliners, rather than risk delay in admission to the school, was suggested. These mothers were unanimous, however, in preferring to have the girls take advantage of the city's educational opportunities, and laid special stress on the work of the school employment bureau, through whose good offices they hoped the dangers of going to improper places of employment might be avoided.

Below is given an analysis of the 38 girls, all taking the dressmaking course, who were studied with regard to their previous training, their record in the Trade School and their home status. The needs for wider opportunities for training and better facilities for placement are clearly indicated, because with the relatively high standard shown by the school records of these girls a wider variety of opportunities than simply dressmaking—a seasonal trade—should have been open to them both in training and placement.

PREVIOUS SCHOOL RECORD

One year in high school	2
Two years in high school	3
Three years in high school	1
Graduated from elementary school	19
Completed 8A grade	3
Completed 7A grade	2
Completed 7B grade	2
Completed 6A grade	2
Completed 6B grade	2
Completed 5B grade	2
Total	38

Twenty-five or 68.9% were graduated from grammar school, or better.
Thirty-two or 84.1% finished 7A, or better.
Thirty-six or 94.7% finished 6A, or better.

AGE ENTERING TRADE SCHOOL

Thirteen to fourteen years	1
Fourteen to fifteen years	2
Fifteen to sixteen years	11
Sixteen to seventeen years	11
Seventeen to eighteen years	7
Eighteen to nineteen years	5
Twenty years	1
Total	38

Rating

Excellent	1
Very good	1
Good to excellent	2
Good	12
Good but slow	5
Fair to good	7
Fair	3
Fair to poor	3
Average	1
Not given	3
Total	38

Home Status

Living with father and mother	21
Living with father	1
Living with mother	12
Living with aunt	1
Living with [not given]	3
Total	38

III. Occupations

Herman Schneider, Dean of the Department of Engineering in the University of Cincinnati and one of the foremost authorities on vocational work in public schools, has in his monograph, "An Analysis of Work," divided labor into two classifications, energizing and devitalizing. He says:

"A highly organized nervous temperament cannot permanently engage in enervating work—*i. e.*, work done over and over again by each worker in the smallest number of cubic feet of space—without making for the breakdown of the individual unless the period of work is shortened sufficiently to permit this worker to engage in some other form of activity which will counteract the effect of his daily occupation. . . . It is fundamental that mankind must do stimulating work or retrogress. This is the bed-rock upon which our constructive programs of education, industry, sociology—of living must rest. . . . One may safely propose as a thesis that only that civilization will prevail whose laws and life conform most nearly to Natural Law. The worth of our education, our laws, our scientific management will be determined by the extent to which they will make clear, conform with and supplement the laws of work. Their test will lie in the degree to which they are useful in leading us safely forward to better, brighter conditions of work and their basic idea must be service to the mass."

He holds thus, that devitalizing tasks make for the breakdown of the individual and the consequent deterioration of the social group engaged in them because of their benumbing effect on the nervous system.

Information concerning the occupations of 200 men and 236 women; fathers, mothers and guardians of the children visited, was secured in the course of this investigation (see Tables XIV and XV). Viewing these occupations in the light of Dean Schneider's analysis, there is to be found among them only a very small percentage of the devitalizing activities which the industrial machine has created but which, for one reason or another, have failed to engage the services of any great number of colored people.

Dean Schneider's illustration of his point—a man who for ten hours a day dropped metal disks into the slot of a stamping machine—has no close analogy among the lists of occupations shown on pages 123 and 124.

The occupation of elevator man, engaging the second largest number in the group, is perhaps the nearest approach to the monotony of the factory hand's work; but the elevator man, on the other hand, has usually alternate night and day shifts of work, he has contact to a greater or less degree with his passengers, and a comparison of his employment with that of the factory-hand is in his favor in all respects excepting that of wages. Few men engaged in industrial work earn as little as $25 or $30 a month, which is the usual wage of elevator men. On the other hand, this wage is almost invariably augmented by tips.

It is noticeable that all the occupations engaging the largest numbers of both men and women are those in which the work is irregular either as to hours or periods of work.

Porters, longshoremen, elevator-men, janitors, among the men; day-workers, dressmakers and seamstresses, among the women, are all in position, to a greater or less degree, to relieve their work by an occasional day of recreation or rest, in contrast with the factory worker's eight or ten hour day or longer period of work from week to week and from month to month.

On the other hand, of course, these irregular hours and days of work make for an instability of income which is especially hard on the women who go out to do day's work, many of them relying on this employment as their sole means of livelihood. Other women find two or three days' work the means of filling in the breach between the husband's insufficient income and the minimum of family necessities.

Some interesting sidelights on the economic situation were furnished by individual cases:

A mother who was sending a daughter through high school, with another younger girl, still in public school, following in her footsteps, was learning to make shirt-waists in a factory during the day and took in laundry work which she and the high school girl did at night.

Another woman, whose husband was a railroad porter, had sent one girl through high school by working at lace curtains. This girl had graduated from the Washington Irving High School and was earning $12.00 a week in a Fifth Avenue dressmaking establishment. The other daughter was taking a course in dressmaking and designing at the Washington Irving High School, and the mother said that the two girls were planning within the next two years to open their own dressmaking establishment.

A girl, graduating at eighteen from public school and refused admission to the Manhattan Trade School, was earning $6 a week as an apprentice in a corsetiere's establishment. Her employer spoke enthusiastically of her ability and faithfulness. The girl's mother was cook in a tea-room but was planning, when the daughter should have become entirely self-supporting, to learn corset-making herself so that they might start their own business.

A boy who had graduated during the year of the investigation was employed as delivery boy for a large shoe-store at $5 a week and was keeping house for his father, a widower, and a younger brother, doing all the cooking, cleaning—everything but the washing and ironing. His father was a longshoreman and the boy could not go to night school or join a club because his father's dinner must be ready between nine and ten o'clock at night.

Another boy washed dishes after school and on Saturday on a dredging boat, to earn money to relieve his mother who was janitress and took in laundry, the father being helpless with asthmatic trouble.

A woman whose daughter was in her first year of high school took in two washings a week, to pay the girl's expenses. The father was butler in a private family and during the summer had no pay except his living expenses. This woman, grizzle-haired and over fifty years old, said that she was attending night school, "so that A (her daughter) won't get away from me."

Although the number of hair-dressers shown in the investigation is small, there are few residence blocks in the colored district without from two to a half dozen establishments for hair-work, massage and baths. Unlike many of their white prototypes these places are not, as a rule, blinds for other less reputable occupations but are the outgrowth of the overwhelming desire of colored women to have their hair straightened and to eke out their own usually short locks with "transformations" of various kinds.

Many of the women in charge of these establishments have private customers among white women. This work, however, is regarded as difficult because of the long hours of standing, in consequence of which many of them are afflicted with broken arches after several years of work; also because of their inability to secure food in restaurants outside the colored districts. Two of these women had become tubercular from long hours of hard work, irregular hours for meals and sometimes inability to get meals at all because they were obliged to fill engagements that left them no time to go to the colored district for dinner or luncheon. The pay, however, is the highest of any earned by colored women, $12 a week being the least amount given by the women from whom inquiries were made.

Among the occupations of the men, the best paid seemed to be those of public porters at railway stations, of longshoremen and of chauffeurs. The earnings of the porters, according to their own statements, ran from $2 to $7 and $9 a day, the latter sums, however, being exceptional. The homes of the men engaged in these occupations were among the most comfortable visited and their wives rarely worked.

Reviewing the whole occupational situation, one feels that the colored men and women are engaged in pursuits that are in themselves more healthful than those of the immigrant population. The domestic character of the women's work makes for training them in keeping their own homes; and the homes in turn reflect this influence by an atmosphere of homelikeness in the majority of them which is rarely found in the same class of homes among other nationalities.

The colored girl seems to adjust herself more readily to the small shop than to the factory. A closer psychological study than it was possible to make in this investigation would be necessary to determine fully the reason for this. The desire for a more personal relation with fellow workers and employers and the greater individual freedom of the small establishment undoubtedly play their part in the problem. Recent graduates of the public schools were found to be engaged as follows:

Girls.

Dressmaking establishments........................ 4
Corset establishments............................. 2
Fur making and modelling.......................... 3
Millinery... 4

Boys.
```
Newspaper route.....................................  I
Florist's establishment (messenger)..................  I
Real estate office (office boy).......................  I
Second assistant drill tender in tunnel...............  I
```

The outlook does not seem unpromising. In spite of the somewhat pessimistic view of principals of trade and high schools, the field of occupations is undoubtedly widening, albeit slowly.

Perhaps rather than toward the factory world of the white man, the future of the colored girl and boy will tend to occupations among their own people, following the race's development through small establishments to large ones.

Already, colored business men have stated, there is a widening field for colored clerks, stenographers, etc., in the colored community; and those interested in a vocational program for colored school children might do well to bear this aspect of the situation in mind.

A canvass of the colored people attending one of the evening schools showed the following occupations among men and women, boys and girls:

Women and Girls.
```
At home—no occupation..........................  53
Housework (general, cooks and waitresses)...........  50
Laundresses.......................................  26
Dressmakers and seamstresses......................  17
Maids (lady's)....................................  13
Stenographers.....................................   4
Milliners.........................................   3
Nurses............................................   2
Office girl.......................................   I
Hairdresser.......................................   I
```

Men and Boys.
```
Porters...........................................  19
Elevator men......................................   6
Tailors...........................................   4
Stock clerks......................................   3
Janitors..........................................   3
Doormen...........................................   2
Bath attendants...................................   2
Machinists........................................   2
Messengers........................................   3
Drivers...........................................   2
Chauffeurs........................................   2
Office boys.......................................   3
```
One each, plumber, deliveryman, valet, fireman, agent, and chair caner.

TABLE XIV.—WOMEN'S OCCUPATIONS (CLASSIFIED)

Domestic	Needle Trades	Business	Miscellaneous
Day's work....97 Laundresses ...30 Housemaids ...27 Cooks........12 Lady's maids .. 7 Boarding and lodging house keepers..... 6 Caretakers .... 4 Care of babies . 1	Dressmakers . 12 Seamstresses . 9	Factory operators 7 Hairdressers ....4 Restaurant keep- ers and caterers 2 Grocery-shop keeper ....1 Asst. in tailor shop.........1 Undertaker .....1 Canvasser for patent medi- cines.........1	Jani- tresses 12 Music teacher .1 Actress ..1
184	21	17	14 Total 236

WOMEN'S OCCUPATIONS

(Arranged according to number in the respective groups)

Day's work	97
Laundresses	30
Housemaids	27
Cooks	12
Janitresses	12
Dressmakers	12
Seamstresses	9
Lady's maids	7
Factory operators	7
Boarding and lodging house keepers	6
Hairdressers	4
Caretakers	4
Restaurant keepers and caterers	2
Music teacher	1
Actress	1
Care of babies	1
Grocer	1
Asst. in tailor shop	1
Undertaker	1
Canvasser for patent medicines	1
Total	236

TABLE XV.—MEN'S OCCUPATIONS (CLASSIFIED)

Unskilled	Skilled	Domestic	Hotel, club or restaurant	Business men	Professional men	Miscellaneous
Head porters ... 2	Chauffeurs ... 6	Coachmen ... 4	Waiters ... 7	Expressmen ... 4	Ministers ... 3	Groc. clerk ... 1
Porters ... 43	Barber ... 1	Butlers ... 4	Cooks ... 9	Coal dealer ... 1	Lawyer ... 1	Assistant weigher custom house ... 1
Elevator men ... 18	Printer ... 1	Housemen ... 2	Steward ... 1	Caterer ... 1	Doctor ... 1	Foreman in coal yard ... 1
Janitors ... 15	Elec. wker. ... 1		Messengers ... 3	Tailors ... 3	Actor ... 1	Asst. shipping clerks ... 2
Longshoremen ... 14	Painters ... 2		Caretaker ... 1	Grocer ... 1	Musicians ... 2	Postal clerk ... 1
Laborers ... 8	Carpenter ... 1		Genl. worker ... 1	Livery ... 1		Picture agts. ... 2
Stablemen ... 3	Engineers ... 2			Farmer ... 1		Salesman's asst. ... 1
Teamsters ... 6	Asst. engineer ... 1					
Street-cleaners ... 2	Bricklayer ... 1					
Asphalt worker ... 1	Plasterer ... 1					
House-cleaner ... 1	Asst. drill tender ... 1					
Furnaceman ... 1	Cigarmakers ... 2					
Steamboat stoker ... 1						
Watchman ... 1						
Bank messengers ... 2						
Washman in laundry ... 1						
119	20	10	22	12	8	9

Total ... 200

MEN'S OCCUPATIONS

(Arranged according to number in the respective groups)

Porters	43	1 each, Asphalt worker
Elevator men	18	House cleaner
Janitors	15	Furnace man
Longshoremen	14	Steamboat stoker
Laborers	8	Watchman
Cooks	9	Washman in laundry
Waiters	7	Barber
Teamsters	6	Printer
Chauffeurs	6	Electric works employe
Coachmen	4	Carpenter
Butlers	4	Asst. engineer
Expressmen	4	Bricklayer
Stablemen	3	Plasterer
Messengers	3	Asst. drill tender
Tailors	3	Steward
Ministers	3	Caretaker
Street cleaners	2	General worker in restaurant
Bank messengers	2	Coal dealer
Painters	2	Caterer
Engineers	2	Grocer
Housemen	2	Liveryman
Musicians	2	Farmer
Asst. shipping clerks	2	Lawyer
Picture agents	2	Doctor
Cigarmakers	2	Actor
		Grocery clerk
		Asst. weigher in custom house
		Foreman in coal yard
		Postal clerk
		Salesman's assistant

The following is a list sent out by the United Colored Democracy during the Municipal Campaign of 1910 and stated to represent the Negroes in the employ of the City of New York.

Assistant District Attorney.
Assistant Corporation Counsel.
Deputy Commissioner of Taxes.
Sealers of Weights and Measures (2).
Sanitary Inspectors (4).
Inspector of Vaults.
Inspector of Licenses.
Corporation Inspectors (5).
Deputy Inspector of Combustibles, Fire Department.
Inspectors of Water Meters (2).
Inspector of Hydrants.
Assistant Engineer, Water Department.
Inspector of Highways.
Inspectors of Disinfectants, Health Department (4).
Inspectors of Mud Scows (2)
Inspector, Tenement House Department.
Detailed Inspector of Garbage.
Stenographers, Dock Department (2).
Stenographer, Department of Highways.
Detailed Foreman, Street Cleaning Department.
Detailed Assistant Foreman, Street Cleaning Department.

First Grade Fireman, Fire Department.
Driver, Fire Department.
Law Clerk, Comptroller's Office.
Clerk, District Attorney's Office.
Clerk, Department of Finance.
Clerk, Tenement House Department.
Clerk, Health Department.
Clerks, Tax Department (2).
Clerks, Department of Docks and Ferries (2).
Clerks, Water Department (2).
Executive Clerk, Mayor's Office.
Patrolmen, Police Department (2).
Assistant Deputy Sheriff, Sheriff's Office.
Clerk, Register's Office, Brooklyn.
Clerk, Coroner's Office, Brooklyn.
Marine Stokers, Department of Docks (6).
Marine Sounder, Department of Bridges.
Confidential Attendant, Corporation Counsel's Office.
Messengers, District Attorney's Office (2).
Messenger, City Chamberlain's Office.
Messenger, Surrogate's Office.
Messenger, Department of Charities.
Messenger, Borough President's Office, Bronx.
Messenger, Water Department.
Elevator Attendant, Borough President's Office.
Cleaners, Sheriff's Office (2).
Cleaner, Department of Highways.
Doormen, Democratic Club (2).
Laborers, Department of Docks and Ferries (25).
Laborers, Park Department (12).
Laborers, Street Cleaning Department (380).
Laborers, Department of Sewers (2).
Laborers, Borough President's Office, Queens.
Laborers, Borough President's Office, Richmond.

IV. Family Incomes

No comprehensive study was made of family incomes. As stated in the first part of the report there was an evident unwillingness on the part of many of the families visited to give information. Only 126 families responded. The incomes are shown in Tables XVI and XVII.

The incomes given are those earned at the time the investigation was made, according to the statements made by the wage-earners. They were said to be fairly representative of the year's work, with the exception of those of the women who earned their living by day's work in private families. These women had little work during the greater part of the summer, and incomes were correspondingly less at that time.

It was found almost invariably that in families where husband and wife were both living, the wife did not work if the husband's income was $12.00 or more a week. If under $12.00, however, the wife worked, at any rate a portion of the time.

TABLE XVI.—FAMILY INCOMES—PER WEEK PER CAPITA

Group	$1	1-1.25	1.26-1.50	1.51-2	2.01-2.50	2.51-3	3.01-3.50	3.51-4	4.01-4.50	4.51-5	5.01-5.50	5.51-6	6.01-6.50	6.51-7	7-
Under-age, 13 families	..	2	2	..	..	5	2	2	..	..	..	..	..	..	..
At-age, 35 families	1	..	3	5	..	6	4	5	5	3	1	1	1	..	..
Over-age, 56 families	2	5	1	6	..	11	8	7	5	3	..	6	..	1	1 $7.50
Exceptional, 22 families	1	2	..	4	..	4	3	2	2	..	..	2	..	1	1 $9.50
Total, 126 families	4	9	6	15	..	26	17	16	12	6	1	9	1	2	2

TABLE XVII.—PER CENT HAVING INCOMES, PER WEEK PER CAPITA

Group	Total No.	Under $2.00		Between $2.00 and $4.50		Over $4.50	
		No.	Per cent	No.	Per cent	No.	Per cent
Over-age	56	14	25.0	31	55.3	11	19.0
Under and at-age	48	13	27.0	29	60.4	6	12.5
Total normal	104	27	25.9	60	57.9	17	16.3
Exceptional	22	7	31.8	11	50.0	4	18.2

The amounts given in the table seemed, in every instance, to be reasonably related to the employment of the wage-earners.

The table indicates that the largest number lay between $1.50 and $4.00 per capita per week, 74 of the total 126 incomes coming within this range; the remaining 52 incomes showed 19 between $1.00 and $1.50 and 28 between $4.00 and $6.00 per capita per week.

The larger per capita incomes were invariably those of small families, father, mother and one child, all steadily employed.

Although the total number of incomes given was too small to afford much pertinent information, an attempt was made to compare the incomes of the families in which there were overage children with those of the families in which there were children at or under age (see Table XVII), and also the incomes of the normal group with those of the exceptional, in order to ascertain, if possible, whether the economic status of the family affected the children's school record. Little can be inferred from the percentages given as the groups form a very small proportion of the original groups studied. This is especially true when we consider the fact mentioned above, namely, that large incomes often mean working children.

PART III

NEEDS AND RECOMMENDATIONS

Ten months of visiting in schools, homes, institutions and other agencies concerned with the development of children, has indicated that the problem of the colored child is two-fold: that it consists not alone in overcoming the difficulties described in the report and so fitting him to live usefully and respectably in the community, but in addition to this in overcoming certain restrictions apparently placed on him because he is colored, for example, in his opportunity to secure employment or in his choice of the neighborhood in which he may live.

The first part of the problem, that which concerns itself with his education and training, appears to be the same on San Juan Hill and Harlem as in the East Side Ghetto and the Italian quarter: *i. e.*, children who have good homes and intelligent parents, especially efficient mothers who remain at home to protect and companion them, show the smallest percentage of departure from the normal in both scholarship and conduct. In fact, so generally has difficulty with the child been found to be coupled with an inefficient mother or with a mother obliged for economic reasons to leave her home for the entire day, that the temptation is strong to ascribe the difficulty almost entirely to lack of home training and care. However, in a number of instances children have made normal progress and behaved themselves with propriety in school when home conditions were everything that was undesirable, and vice versa.

This part of the problem is an individual one, as each troublesome child requires careful study and adjustment in many directions. No generality has been found applicable to even a small group of children and therefore while playgrounds may be multiplied and the methods of conducting them improved; while day nursery activities may be elaborated even to making possible co-operation with the public schools; or Big Brothers and Big Sisters, Boy Scouts, Camp Fire Girls, clubs and classes, etc., may be developed on the one hand, and the curriculum of the school changed on the other, it is unlikely that the child who presents an unusual problem will be reached unless some one person with the ability to judge reactions can give to that child a large amount of time and sympathetic attention.

The second part of the problem, that part which exists for the colored child because he is colored, does not seem possible of solution so long as public opinion continues to find itself unable to come to a decision on the question of whether the negro race should or should not be under a separate régime in the social fabric. And because of this race feeling or opinion (sometimes both), emotions are aroused which in their action and counter-action have created an endless chain of discrimination, grading from indifference and neglect to active persecution. The very social forces working in behalf of the handicapped of other race, are in many instances not available for colored people. Those most strongly affected by this state of affairs are naturally the least developed and most defenseless members of this least de-veloped of all the races composing our polyglot population, and it is therefore difficult to say with justice, when lapses from stand-ards are encountered, where individual disability stops and where community responsibility commences.

After all, we are only beginning dimly to comprehend human problems and to evolve from one angle or another methods of dealing with them. The most we can do for the colored child is to give him whatever is found sufficiently good to offer to other children, and the least we can do for him is to give him the benefit of every force now being employed to enhance the well being of all children.

I. School Needs

As the intensive study, reinforced by the findings of the pre-liminary survey, points out, the two most pressing problems of the children in the elementary schools are over age, *i. e.*, retarda-tion, and irregular attendance, the latter difficulty often being the cause of the former. Various means within the schools have been tried in order to overcome these difficulties; it is possible that the same remedy applied to both ills outside the school, but in full co-operation with it, would accomplish much.

1. Over-age.—The large percentage of over-age shown by the study—a percentage out of all proportion to that given in the report of the City Superintendent for the year ending July 31,

1913, for the schools of New York as a whole—renders most significant the step taken toward promotion by subject, and the installation of double periods in reading, writing and arithmetic which were inaugurated for over-age boys in Public School 89 in the fall of 1913. Two hundred boys in grades 3B, 4A, 4B, 5A and 5B were given two periods of reading and arithmetic instead of one, in the grade work for which they were best equipped. The result after two months showed that ten of these boys were returned to their grades and the others exhibited such marked improvement that the principal was inclined to think this problem was in a fair way of being solved. Not only was the boys' scholarship improved, but their conduct, attention and general morale were noticeably better. There has been no further opportunity to follow up the records of the pupils working under this plan as it was inaugurated only two months prior to the close of this investigation. The principal of Public School 89 was enthusiastic in his estimate of the effect of the work on both the scholarship and conduct of the boys, and Dr. Frank Bachman when consulted concerning this experiment spoke of its great possibility for usefulness in all schools containing 6th, 7th and 8th grades. If the plan has proved successful, its general use by the school authorities is urged in coping with this over-age condition.

The life of the child outside the school, however, furnishes the main reason for this evil of retardation. In all the districts studied the greatest cause is undoubtedly the lack of care of the children whose parents, for whatever reason, do not give them adequate companionship and guidance,—the problem that is everywhere coming to be considered one of the greatest of those affecting the mass of the population. These children, whether of the families of working parents or of ignorant or immoral or neglectful parents, or of widowed or deserted mothers, are as yet untouched by any community scheme, whether churches, settlements, day nurseries, school centers, etc., because all of these activities deal with children en masse and none, so far as can be discovered, study the child as an individual. If he is not interested or does not attend these activities the burden of blame rests on him or on his parents or guardians. The reaction of the child's individual preferences is apparently not taken into account.

It has been shown fairly conclusively that the settlement clubs and other activities do not—and undoubtedly cannot—give this individual care. The work of the settlement as an institution makes it impossible for the workers to adjust the hours for the various activities to the needs of each child. Day nurseries would need to be multiplied many times beyond their present number—and in fact beyond the legitimate need for the peculiar service they render—if they were equipped to cope adequately with the problem of the uncared-for child of school age.

The School Recreation Center would seem to be the logical means of providing this care. Not the recreation center as it is now organized, with incomplete equipment, an insufficient, untrained force and haphazard attendance; but a center based on an accurate knowledge of the needs of the school population and worked out through a careful canvass of the homes in order to learn specifically which of the children require care and to secure the authority of parents to keep those children in safe custody until called for at the school; a center which should make arrangements with class-room teachers for receiving the children after their school tasks are completed, and which should devote its program to activities that develop definite, healthy means of self-expression in each child as well as protecting him from the unguided, haphazard street life that now occupies all his waking hours spent away from school-room lessons.

It has been suggested that widows' pensions would, by enabling women to remain in their homes, obviate the necessity for this community care of children. The study has shown, however, that the children of widows form only a small percentage of the total number of children requiring this care; and, more often than not, the insufficient earnings of the father make it necessary for the mother to be a wage-earner. Even if the limitations of race did not tie colored men to unprofitable occupations in the majority of cases, few of these men would be able in any occupation to earn a sufficient wage to support a family. Industrial conditions in the community as a whole are rendering it difficult, if not impossible, for one wage earner to support a family in decent comfort, and therefore the pensioning of widowed mothers would relieve only a small percentage of the enforced neglect of children because of economic necessity. Furthermore, economic necessity is not the sole reason for neglect; it is sad but true that numerous maldevelopments are plainly shown to be due to parental inefficiency, incompatibility and misunderstanding.

Looking at the problem as one that concerns itself with the best means of dealing with the child whose home life, for whatever reason, is not making for his proper development, a school center of the character mentioned seems to afford a promise of relief. Public School 28, located as it is in a district about equally divided between vice and poverty, having few social agencies of any sort and none for colored school children, has suggested itself as an excellent place for inaugurating a center of this nature. The principal of the school was keenly interested in the plan, and the director of the Hudson Guild offered co-operation. In consideration of the peculiar service it was proposed to render, the school would probably afford a better location than would a church or a private agency for such a center, as the parents of all the school children might thus be reached untrammelled by affiliations of any nature.

The vital points of the work of the center would of course be the definite care given and definite responsibility assumed for the children from the time they were taken from their classrooms until they were called for by their parents or guardians. The activities might range from walking and swimming clubs, as already organized in many of the schools, to basket-ball or baseball teams, singing, cooking or sewing classes, study rooms, arrangements for medical and dental care, etc. As the plan contemplates care of the children on every school day and on Saturdays, if necessary, each child would require naturally a variety of activities.

Those with whom the plan was discussed thought it held promise of aiding definitely in the prevention of much juvenile delinquency, and made for building normal, well-trained children from those who might otherwise become the street waifs or the lonely shut-ins. This last group of children, lacking companionship and guidance, many of them without even ordinary facility of speech as a means of self-expression, this study has found to be the victims of the solitude, non-development or wrong development resulting from parental neglect,—whether that neglect was brought about by economic necessity or by other causes.

Of equal importance in dealing with this question of lack of home care is the Visiting Teacher, without whose co-operation it would be difficult, if not indeed impossible, to develop the center just described.

In spite of the feeling by certain students of school problems that the visiting teacher is a superfluity and that all difficulties arising with school children can be adjusted by a principal who possesses social consciousness and knowledge of community resources and who works in co-operation with class teachers, attendance officers, school doctors and nurses, and parents, there remains the fact that at present in only one of the schools studied was there any approach to this "team work"; and that even the very excellent work done there did not tie up those loose ends in the children's lives caused by the lack of parental care from early morning until bed-time. None of the social agencies in the district were available for the close-knit co-operation necessary to care properly for these children, and none provided a place where the children might be retained until their parents or guardians called for them.

The results secured from individual cases referred to the social agencies were not encouraging, and unless a radical change is finally brought about in the following up of these individual cases and in methods of dealing with them it would seem that, in addition to a school recreation center, visiting teachers were necessary both in the Chelsea and San Juan Hill districts and in Harlem.

The situation would probably best be met at present by the addition of several visiting teachers to the staff of the Public Education Association. It has been suggested that the West End Workers' Association and the Chelsea Neighborhood Association might be asked to join in raising the $1,000 or $1,200 a year necessary to provide such workers in their districts.

In Harlem it has been suggested that the Urban League might raise the necessary funds among the churches and other social agencies in that district. This latter plan may not be a wise one, however, as the Urban League is definitely committed to a policy of employing and training colored workers and it seems to the investigator that for this particular service the time is not yet ripe for a colored worker in Harlem. For many forms of social service a colored worker would, doubtless, be as successful as a white one; but present conditions demanding training and long experience on the part of the worker and a place of authority in relation to the schools have seemed to indicate the advisability of employing white visiting teachers. It is rightly maintained that colored people must be taught to respect social workers of their own race, and after the relation between the homes and the schools has been established and a better understanding has been brought about it may well be that a colored worker can more advantageously be employed. At present it is the opinion of the investigator that the situation, so far as the welfare of the child is concerned, is in danger of being sacrificed to the plan of training colored social workers.

2. Truancy.—The second important problem in connection with colored school children has been truancy and irregular attendance.

The intensive study points out, however, that truancy exists in this group only to a slightly greater degree than in the entire school population. It may be that the consequences of truancy are more serious with these children because of the difficult home conditions that prevail among them. In any case, whether or not the problem is greater here than in other districts of the city, it is sufficiently serious to justify recommending measures for meeting it. In connection with this problem the investigation brought to light what appears to be pertinent information.

In the first place, at 34 of the addresses given on the school cards no knowledge of the child or family could be secured; and 22 more had moved and could not be found. The time lost in looking up new addresses might be saved if the correct address of each child were secured and verified at the beginning of each term or oftener. The co-operation of older pupils of proven reliability, and of alumni associations might be of value here.

This question of attendance is also immediately affected by parental neglect, indeed is almost identical with the general problem of the child who is neglected or improperly guarded at home, and the same remedies, therefore, can be applied. Probably no more significant fact has been developed by the study than that *in not one single instance* were normal home surroundings found in the group of truant boys studied, and by normal home surroundings nothing less is meant than a home in which both parents were living, the father working and the mother remaining at home to care for the children. The method of taking no account of home conditions in the reports made by the attendance officer cannot fail to leave this problem unsolved, especially in the more aggravated cases of non-attendance.

In no department, perhaps, is the good effect of the visiting teacher's work shown more distinctly than in dealing with cases of incipient truancy, and it is just here that sustained effort brought to bear on individual cases is of the highest importance. The attendance officer, attached as he is to the schools of an entire district, cannot, as a rule, give the necessary time for solving the individual problems involved. Those attendance officers who have become successful social influences with the truants in their districts have usually been unsuccessful in handling a sufficiently large number of cases to cover the districts adequately. In one large school 500 out of 2,500 pupils had been reported for truancy during one school year and the problem was so acute it almost seemed to warrant the attachment of an attendance officer to this school exclusively. The difficulties arising from truancy conditions here, together with the unwillingness of teachers to visit the homes; and the unpleasant relations existing between another school and some of the homes of its colored pupils, all called for the help of the visiting teacher.*

In the smaller schools, like Public Schools 100 and 141, the principal and head of department have practically been visiting teachers, and might easily acquire a sufficient familiarity with the social agencies available for help in meeting the problems that arise in connection with non-attendance cases. In the larger schools, however, the human side of the problem has not been adequately dealt with, and much ill will has resulted on the part of every one concerned. Social service and close follow-up work are needed here just as surely as they are needed for the patient leaving a hospital; a teacher or a school principal should not be expected to give such service any more than are the nurse and hospital superintendent.

Local school boards might well interest themselves in the work, and in co-operation with alumni associations might render vital aid.

School luncheons would undoubtedly help, especially in Public Schools 89 and 68, in dealing with the attendance problem, as many of the children who go home to prepare their own lunches fail to return in the afternoon. If luncheons were available at school an understanding might be effected with parents whereby the children needing luncheons would be kept in school during the noon recess. There is an open air playground in P. S. 89 where the children of this school, who constitute the largest percentage of the problem, might have outdoor exercise at noontime.

The large percentage of colored children who are required to care for younger brothers and sisters after school hours, or who are kept from school to give this care, render desirable the formation in all the schools studied of the Little Mothers' Leagues organized by the Bureau of Child Hygiene of the City Department of Health. On the application of the principal of any school a

* Some of these difficulties will be met if the plans of the new Bureau of Attendance are carried out.

nurse is assigned by the Bureau of Child Hygiene to organize the League, and all the year round, summer and winter, the children are instructed by nurses and doctors from the Department of Health in various phases of child caring. These Leagues have been of incalculable value in the East Side schools in which they have been organized, not only because of their educational aspect but because of their salutary effect on the discipline and general morale of their membership. Many an Italian and Jewish mother has found herself confronted on the recreation pier or in the park by an indignant Little Mothers' Leaguer, flourishing a small admonishing finger under the nose of the merely grown-up, but woefully ignorant woman, with the demand: "Say, don't you know no better nor to give that baby lollipops? Say, do you want to kill him before he's got a chance?"

A Parental School for Girls seems to be in every way desirable. So much of the trouble with the children in court cases was found to be rooted in non-attendance that if the first offenders were dealt with by a parental school it would seem that more serious trouble might be averted, especially in cases where working mothers cannot discipline incipient truants in a sufficiently strenuous manner to obviate the difficulty. In the case of the inefficient and immoral mother a commitment for improper guardianship would naturally be in order; but many cases of waywardness in the daughters of working mothers undoubtedly would have been checked on the safe side of actual immorality, if a parental school had been available.

Mothers' meetings would undoubtedly help with this problem, but those held in the afternoon have not been successful because of the large proportion of working mothers, and the idea of evening meetings has not met with favor by the principals or teachers. An outside agency might undertake to develop these evening meetings but here again rises the question of inaugurating any activity exclusively for colored people in the public schools.

In Philadelphia, the Armstrong Association's school visitor organized several remarkably successful groups of colored women, holding the meetings in the members' homes and keeping each group small enough to make this possible. Noticeably good results were secured in developing the women themselves and in eliminating many of the difficulties in the school with the children.

With the opening of a social center in the school these groups were consolidated into a larger body which now meets in the school building; but the young woman in charge of the work stated that she felt much of the social spirit had been lost in the merging of the clubs and the transfer to the school building, although the problems of the children were more adequately presented and discussed.

It might be possible through the efforts of the visiting teachers to promote school meetings in the evening even though class teachers did not participate in the meetings. Most, if not all, of the principals would take real interest in such meetings.

The lack of proper care of children by their parents or other guardians has been found to lie at the root of so large a percentage of all the problems arising in school that one is almost tempted to ask that failure to give such care be made a penal offense. If a parent fails to clothe or feed or if he brutally beats a child, the law reaches him effectively. If, however, he is merely very industrious or over-indulgent and the spiritual and mental growth of the child suffer quite as severely as does his body in the other cases, it is difficult, often impossible, to secure for the child his right to a "fair chance" to develop into a normal human being. The colored child, because of his strong native instinct for social relationship, is particularly in need of sympathetic individual attention. Club leaders and teachers in the settlements, as well as in the schools, have remarked on the fact that colored children require a greater amount of personal consideration than do the white children with whom they come in contact and most of them agree that loneliness has much to do with this.

3. Weakened Mentality.—The noticeable tendency to mental abnormalities at the age of adolescence requires a closer study than it was possible to make during the period of this investigation, and the Committee is urged to give this matter consideration. It has been suggested that the National Association for the Advancement of Colored People might wish to coöperate if it should be decided to pursue the matter further.

It was not thought advisable by the Public Education Association's executive staff, when the investigation was planned, to make psychological tests of the mental calibre of the pupils studied, but rather to gauge the extent to which such tests might be necessary. The study of the troublesome children showed the necessity for careful consideration of environment and home training, especially in the border-line mental cases; also the nice distinction that must be drawn between mental and moral defect

4. Vocational Training and Guidance.—In close connection with the problems within the school, especially in relation to high and trade schools, exists the very important need of providing more adequately not alone for training for work, but also for placing in situations the colored boys and girls who graduate from the public schools or who are for any reason whatever leaving school when they are legally permitted to do so.

The study has indicated plainly that there is a field for colored workers in the industries; but it has also indicated that in the trade schools there is race discrimination on the part of the authorities and, especially, that the applications of colored girls for admission to the Manhattan Trade School are not always considered in the order in which they are made. In view of the fact that a number of girls from one school had failed to secure admission to the Trade School it would seem to be in order to have the question of eligibility of colored girls definitely passed upon by the school authorities. This question might well be referred to the National Association for the Advancement of Colored People which is concerning itself with all matters relating to the civil status of Negroes. The eligibility to admission to a public school is surely such a question and one of great importance.

A much more comprehensive knowledge of the occupations open to colored boys and girls would be available if an endeavor could be made in connection with grammar and high schools to obtain information for at least two years after leaving school concerning the work secured by the boys and girls who either graduate, or who secure working papers before graduation. This information might then be placed at the disposal of the employment bureaus of both boys' and girls' trade schools. There is so much discouragement for these boys and girls in their efforts to make a place for themselves that any light on their problems would surely make worth while even a considerable amount of additional expense and work.

It has also suggested itself that the evening trade schools might be helped very materially in placing their pupils by cooperation with the vocational bureaus of the day trade schools. None of the evening trade schools have had systematic placement arrangements, although their need for such service is obvious.

Very definite recommendations as to summer studies, especially for first year high school students, would be of the greatest value to these boys and girls. Some volunteer association, for instance, the National League on Urban Conditions Among Negroes, might find it desirable to discuss this matter with high school principals in order to secure from them information and advice concerning the specific pupils who require summer tutoring or study classes, and whom they might assist in procuring such help.

Several workers have urged the necessity for a school of domestic science to train colored girls in housework. It is a question whether colored girls should be trained for housework in preference to any other means of livelihood, for other occupations are undoubtedly opening more and more broadly and they should rather be given their choice of an occupation for which they feel they are fitted. The large number of colored people attending the night schools shows an increasing tendency on the part of the working population to make the best use of their leisure time; and the lack of time for improvement as well as for recreation undoubtedly lies at the root of the growing unwillingness to go into domestic service, together with the disadvantage, as many of them have said, of "not being with my own kind." "No one knows, Miss," one girl said, "how hard it is, where there is only one in help, to be by yourself all the time and never talk about things you want to." Whether for good or evil, this is the cry of the house servant, colored and white, and the testimony from both girls and their parents does not encourage a belief in the success of a school to train housemaids if it were established.

5. Race Feeling.—In the consideration of the public school's relationship to the problem of the colored child it is not possible to ignore the matter of race feeling. While the majority of the teachers showed much sympathy and kindly feeling for their colored pupils there was undoubted evidence in some cases of active dislike, and it has been noticeable that the principals who have most successfully coped with this problem are those who have insisted that no mention ever be made of color. One principal told me that the salutary effect on the teachers' attitude of this ruling made by her had been marked, and she felt that if principals would consistently insist that no such term as "Negro" or "colored" be used in discussing their pupils, much improvement would be secured.

II. Social Needs

Aside from the need existing in the public schools to meet adequately the problem of the colored school child, perhaps the correctional institutions have the most immediate bearing on the problem. The State Training School for delinquent girls should undoubtedly be enlarged and at once, and every effort should be made to make a place there at least for a colored girl of school age who has become a mother or has been found to have lapsed sexually. It seems a great pity that girls who have had experiences of this nature should return to the public schools and mingle with innocent children. The girls found in this study to have had such experiences had not in a single instance been ignorantly and innocently led astray, and there is no doubt that every one of them would be benefited by the discipline of institutional life with definite training for a period of at least several years.

If Hudson Training School is growing unwieldy in size, then the question arises whether there shall be a second institution for colored girls or, preferably, one for rural cases. In the second alternative, the course of training might be arranged to fit the girls for the kind of life they would return to after leaving the institution, aside from the fact that rural and urban cases probably differ in nature more vitally than do the white and colored cases.

Since the foregoing matter indicates a wide diversity of opinion on the problem of the delinquent colored girl, not only by the state authorities but also by philanthropic organizations interested in the question, it would seem advisable that a public conference be called with a view to discussing the advisability of additional accommodations for colored girls in the State Training School on the one hand; and on the other hand, the relative value of establishing a home for delinquent colored girls or a training school for girls who are not delinquent, as Miss Davis has suggested.

In 1914 there was accommodation for fifty girls in the House of the Good Shepherd Country Home, while only thirty-one had then been committed. If the Protestant Mission societies will parallel this extension of the Catholics' work, and will take care of Protestant cases not eligible to Hudson or which it is not thought best to send there, the community scheme for correctional work should be fairly complete.

There is a real opportunity here for some agency interested in the colored race to perform the service which is already being undertaken by other races, of supplying a friendly visitor from New York to visit the Hudson Training School or other correctional institutions periodically, perhaps giving the girls religious instruction but at any rate gaining a friendly footing with them and helping with their care when their probationary period arrives. The Council of Jewish Women has paid visitors who are performing this service for Jewish girls both at Hudson and at the Bedford Reformatory, and the value of their work has been publicly endorsed by the authorities of both institutions.

The need of a parental school for girls has been spoken of, and in the cases of girls too young for commitment to Hudson or of school girls whose offenses do not seem to warrant such severe punishment and whose parents seem unable to cope with the situation, such special school would undoubtedly be of real constructive help with both white and colored truants and juvenile delinquents.

There is need for a public playground in Harlem and if the owners of the numerous vacant lots would give permission to have them used, the recreation committee of the Board of Education or some other public or private agency might be induced to equip them. This would fill the need for playgrounds until the Board of Estimate and Apportionment could be prevailed upon to make a purchase for that purpose.

The property adjoining Public School 100, at the corner of Fifth Avenue and 138th Street, was unoccupied at the time this report was made, as were a number of lots in the middle of the block between Lenox and Fifth Avenues. Any one of these properties is in a more congested neighborhood than the property already suggested to the Board of Estimate and Apportionment between Lenox and Seventh Avenues and could probably be bought at a figure considerably lower than that asked for property considered by them. It might also be possible to secure permission of the owners of these lots to use them, so long as they remained unsold, for playgrounds equipped in the manner suggested above. This has been done in numerous instances in other parts of the city.*

It is hoped that a strong effort will be made to induce the police department to check the growth of petty as well as of graver criminal offenses in the Harlem district; here also efficient aid might be secured through visiting the homes of the school children. If the social agencies in Harlem were organized, and if it were made known that a body of workers existed through whom complaints requiring police action might be pushed, it would no doubt be possible to improve conditions in Harlem as they have been improved on the lower West Side.

* Cf. p. 75, indicating that such action has already been successfully undertaken as a result of this suggestion.

So far as the colored school child is concerned, it is a difficult matter to make a résumé of needs that may be met by agencies supported by private philanthropy. With few exceptions those now in existence have met with little response. The children studied in this investigation show an almost infinitesimal percentage of affiliation with any philanthropically supported body, and those who are members of clubs, classes, etc., do not attend regularly.

Information gleaned from parents and teachers as well as children themselves, indicates that this non-attendance is not due primarily to indifference or neglect on the part of the children and their parents but rather to the fact that the majority of children, both boys and girls, are busy with household tasks, errands, and in the case of the boys, with regular employment. The minor, rather than the major reason for non-attendance seems to be the failure of the activities offered to strike a responsive chord in the breasts of the would-be beneficiaries.

It has been pointed out that these colored children are apt to respond to a real and practical need, and to attend activities closely connected with their immediate home surroundings. In the neighborhoods where living conditions are particularly bad —as in San Juan Hill and parts of Harlem—one wonders why social agencies of the neighborhood should be worrying about inducing children to come to cooking classes, sewing classes and clubs when there is so much need for inculcating the first principles of citizenship in keeping departments up to their duties. Waring Juvenile Leagues to see that the streets are kept clean, Little Mothers' Leagues to see that the babies are kept clean, and a Junior Tenement House Reform League to see that the houses are kept clean and habitable might interest the children, whereas other activities have so far failed to hold them.

Principals, teachers and parents were almost unanimous in their condemnation of evening clubs for girls, or even for boys who were in school. Those children who were being intelligently brought up were, as a rule, given their recreation in the afternoon, whether that recreation meant moving pictures, base-ball, tennis clubs, or what not; and employed their evenings in studying, with an early retiring hour.

The less fortunate children played on the street, both afternoon and evening, but no parents were discovered who were willing to consent to have girls, at any rate, attend evening clubs.

The experience of a number of club leaders, who had found in dance halls and other undesirable places girls who were supposed to be in their clubs, would seem to bear out this objection, especially in view of the fact that these same girls had never previously been permitted to go out at night unaccompanied by their parents or other relatives.

Undoubtedly there is need for providing more wholesome activities for younger boys and girls than are now provided for by social agencies. Twelve years is the youngest age at which children are admitted to clubs; whereas incipient truants and delinquents—especially children who have no home care—develop vagrant habits at the age of seven or eight, and even at ten years of age it is difficult to correct those habits. The need for afternoon activities should therefore be emphasized, and for the younger as well as the older children.

Continuous, close knit, personal and individual work with parents and children is undoubtedly required, as well as attention to the recreational activities in relation with the personal preferences of the children.

Lack of discipline lies so vitally and palpably at the root of most of the troublesome cases (where children have normal mentality) that a factor in the success of any work would undoubtedly be the co-operation of those having authority over the children. One method of securing such co-operation is that used by the Henry Street Settlement where a child is never accepted into membership of one of the clubs until the parents or guardians have been formally visited and their consent gained. The child is therefore aware that his recreation is not a free-lance affair but has the cognizance and approval of those who have authority over him.

Probably much of the lack of success in holding boys and girls in clubs is due to the personality and methods of the workers. New York, without a doubt, has less really good material among its colored social workers than can be found in many other cities, though there are striking exceptions to this fact. One reason for this may be the larger salaries paid elsewhere as well as the more sharply defined character of the colored population in other cities. In New York the colored population is made up of almost as polyglot and shifting a composition as is our white population. The social fabric of the colored population, too, just emerging as it is from a democracy that formerly had no elements of social caste, is beginning already to develop a lack of sympathy between those whose intelligence fits them to help and the strata most in need of development, because of the false value placed on purely intellectual attainments by some members of the group who have desired or obtained a higher mental training.

The most successful hold on the boys and girls of the poorer and least developed parents, was, I found, not that of the professionally or quasi-professionally trained social worker, but rather the influence of the less developed church and Sunday School workers who were teaching the children playlets, "pieces to speak" and other features of Sunday School and church entertainments. These features were not as artistic nor did they have the educational influence of cooking and sewing classes and club activities offered by the regularly organized social centres. Nevertheless, the church "sister" who, it seemed, never ceased her activities in "getting up" church socials and Sunday School entertainments, was the one who held her girls and boys—she called for them and took them back to their homes from rehearsals. There was a bond of sympathy between her and her young people that was rarely seen elsewhere. In home after home Loretta, or Avice, or Fred, or William was found so congenially occupied with these activities that the lack of cooking or dressmaking or carpentry class or gymnasium never suggested itself.

The love of self-expression—but self-expression on the plane of their own development—is doubtless the mainspring of the interest here. As Mrs. Johnson of St. Cyprian's Parish House wisely said, "if social workers would only bear in mind the development of a harmonious personality and not try all at once to lift a human being from the depths to the heights in 'spots,' leaving the various segments of his psychology at war with each other, a more successful hold might be secured." Without doubt, it requires a highly developed worker to make the proper distinctions, but this worker also felt that much of the lack of success in reaching individuals lay in a failure to understand this point.

Too much emphasis cannot be laid on the fact that much, almost everything, in the case of colored children depends upon the personal influence exerted by the head worker, club leader, or whoever comes most in contact with the children. This may account, often does, for a failure to respond to recreational activities no matter how generously provided. A genial atmosphere and freedom from the disciplinary features of the classroom should bring about success in securing regular attendance.

In the course of the investigation different groups of young men and women were met who seemed to offer very valuable material for social workers, either professional or volunteer. These were the members of various church societies, the groups of girls connected with the Y. W. C. A. and some high school boys and girls. If the National League on Urban Conditions Among Negroes should in its development of social workers, find it possible to offer a prize of a college scholarship for some particularly excellent social service by the young men and women in these church societies, the time seems to be ripe for an experiment of this nature. A scholarship in college might also be offered to high school boys and girls as a prize for exceptional social service. A plan has been under consideration to offer a scholarship in the high schools, but the wisdom of this seems questionable in view of the fact that a decided feeling exists among the colored boys and girls of high school age against anything that would tend to differentiate them as a group in the schools. One girl had so keenly resented a teacher's reference to the good record made by the colored girls of her class, because they had been referred to as colored, that she had with difficulty been induced to return to school. To a less extent the same feeling existed in many other of the colored pupils and for this reason it would doubtless be wiser to offer the scholarship in outside organizations, under the auspices of a properly qualified committee.

The need for settlement clubs and for similar activities as shown in the respective districts studied is a diversified one. In the San Juan Hill district a center is about to be developed by the Stillman House branch of the Henry Street Settlement in the house now occupied jointly by the Free Kindergarten Association for Colored Children and the Lincoln Day Nursery.*

The Stillman House authorities and workers have felt in the past that they were not successful in holding the boys and girls in clubs. Probable reasons for this have been pointed out, and as the lack of recreational facilities is the great lack on San Juan Hill, if the new center lays the greatest stress upon recreational features it may do much for the neighborhood. The gymnasium at St. Cyprian's, as has been stated, was not being used to its capacity, yet there was great need on San Juan Hill for such an activity. It might be that Stillman House could help in developing this gymnasium.

* This has been done. See Appendix II.

Stillman House in its plan to take over the building occupied by the Lincoln Day Nursery proposed to discontinue the Nursery. The large percentage of poor school attendance, especially among girls, and the cause in many instances of their leaving school before graduation, has been shown to be due to the fact that they have been needed at home to aid in caring for the younger children. Day nurseries are not an ideal way of meeting this need, yet in the present scheme of industrial life some method of caring for children of working mothers is likely to be more instead of less necessary, since the trend of affairs takes mothers out of their homes to an increasingly large extent. If a nursery or other method for such care is efficiently managed there is surely a greater promise that the children will receive better care than if they are left to the irresponsible, unsupervised care of needy neighbors at a much higher cost. (The price usually asked for this care is twenty-five cents per day; and for children too young to be able to tell of neglect or ill-treatment it is a hazardous method.) Any large center doing neighborhood work might well extend its activities to include care for the children of school age as well as the babies in the families on its lists, where mothers are away from home. This after-care of school children is part of the plan of some of the East Side day nurseries but has not thus far been undertaken by the nurseries for colored children, except in a most informal and undeveloped way.

If it is desirable to continue the maintenance of day nurseries, an effort should surely be made by the management to go out after its neighborhood problem. This might be done through co-operation with the principals and attendance officers of the schools, with the relief giving agencies and with the churches. There was no opportunity to make a study of the families using the Lincoln Day Nursery and therefore no comparison could be made between their needs and those of the families with whom the school investigation was concerned. The problem of the nursery is, however, intimately connected with the problem of attendance in the schools, and if a nursery could be conducted in connection with a milk station and after-school care provided for the children of school age on the nursery's register, a program of social education of the families might be worked out. The superintendent of such a nursery should have the definite training of the nurses at the milk stations, or the assistance of such nurses; and by combining the day nursery with the milk station plus a playground, study room and other activities for children of school age, a really efficient center might be the result. If such a center could be developed by Stillman House in its new home, the neighborhood activities of San Juan Hill would present a more rounded-out program. Or such need would be met if the Board of Managers of St. Cyprian's, with a milk station already established and with three houses available for activities, should see their way to develop such a center, although it would probably have a better chance for success if it were non-sectarian. St. Cyprian's milk station too, as previously stated, is not affiliated with the association of milk stations and does not have the educational features in the form of mothers' meetings, house to house visiting by the nurses, etc., that form so valuable a feature of the milk stations conducted by the Department of Health.

An indirect method of partly meeting this need of after-school care for children and all day care for babies would be the organization of a desertion bureau, such as the Jewish community carries on. Fewer women might be obliged to leave their homes with the resulting bad effects on the neglected children if their absent husbands could be compelled to pay toward their support.

In Harlem, social workers among the colored people feel that a settlement house is needed. But unless such an organization succeeds in bringing about far closer co-operation than at present exists between the home, the school and the social agencies of this district, it is not probable that anything having a vital bearing on the problem of the colored child will result. The private agencies are too apt to look on such co-operation purely as it relates to the problem of the school or of the agency involved, and not as it relates to the problem of the child.

The school social center seems to bear far more promise of success in dealing with the difficulties of school children than an additional private agency, since the agencies already in existence have for some reason failed to check the evils of truancy and its resultant bad habits in both boys and girls.

The Music School Settlement meets some of the social needs felt in Harlem and might meet still more. It has been suggested that its leader might extend the field of the settlement influence by arranging with the better grade moving picture and vaudeville theatres in the Harlem district to devote musical programs during certain periods in the week or month to Negro music of the better grade interpreted by Negro artists, featuring such programs on their bills.   In this way the Music School Settlement might influence a wider audience than it could attract to its own center, and would accomplish its work in a more normal manner.

Concerts in Public Schools 100, 89, 119 and 68 might prove as attractive in Harlem as they have in other localities.   In fact, so successful has this form of amusement proved in Brooklyn and on the lower East Side, that it would seem as though Harlem were somewhat backward in adopting the plan.   Such concerts would not, by any means, need to be given exclusively or continually by or for the colored people, but Negro music and Negro musicians might have an adequate representation in the program of these schools as well as elsewhere in the city.

Money expended in promoting such a plan would reach a larger and more constantly widening number of beneficiaries than would the same amount invested in a new plant for the music school and its upkeep.

The third district studied, that between 34th and 42nd Streets, running from Seventh Avenue to North River, offers a clear field for activities for colored people, for, except the colored mission at 30th Street, south of this district, there was no organized social activity for colored people.   It has been suggested that a milk station might be established in this district from which might grow mothers' meetings and the possibility of clubs, etc., for children.

The plan for a social center outlined in the recommendations for school activities affords the best sort of opportunity for reaching the children of the neighborhood and would be of great service in this barren section.

There was evidence, too, for need of improved police service in this district.   The suggested conference on the co-operation between social agencies, the police department and the health department would without doubt have an important bearing on the situation in this district as well as elsewhere.

Summary

To summarize the special needs with which we are confronted on finishing this report: It seems clear that the needs of the colored school child who is backward or delinquent come chiefly from a wrong home environment, or from lack of care.   These wrong home conditions usually result in retardation or truancy or both.   A cure can come only by careful attention to individual problems.   One way of giving this attention would be through a socialized school recreation center and enough visiting teachers to connect this center with the homes, or to deal with the cases where there is no such center. School lunches and mothers' clubs would also help greatly. In the question of truancy, a careful assignment of truant officers and a parental school for girls are much needed.

In order to bring about better relations within the schools greater care needs to be exercised by principals and teachers with regard to race feeling or its expression. Further effort needs to be made with regard to training for industry and finding promising positions for the children who have been trained. As to the work of social agencies, if more definite knowledge of the home conditions and school standing of the children attending clubs and classes were acquired by social workers who are endeavoring to form these clubs or classes, a better correlation between outside activities and both home and school needs would without doubt follow.

More facilities for the care of delinquent girls are needed, as well as better plans for recreation and follow-up work to prevent such delinquency. In the matter of health everything is still to be done, both in school and out, and more attention should be paid by teachers to school problems caused by ill health, by social agencies to fresh air work and after-school care, and by public departments to co-operation both with schools and social agencies on matters of health.

Among the general needs brought out by this report seems to be the one of raising the standard with regard to sex morality among these children and their parents. But before judging that to be a greater need here than in any other congested quarter of the city or less developed community, it is interesting to note various opinions on the subject. It is peculiarly true of this problem of sex morality that it is discussed as a Negro problem, a Jewish problem, etc., when it is truly a universal problem, as the following instance will show. Several years ago, the opinion of a white woman who had worked among the more ignorant of the southern colored people, was asked on the growth of conventional marriage relations among them. She said, "I believe I can best express the condition of affairs by stating that the girls with whom we have been working have come to feel that it is respectable to be married at least a short time before their babies are born." Two years ago, while the investigator was in the Hawaiian Islands, a Bishop there, who had had what amounts to a father's part in rearing the native girls attached to his diocese, was asked how he regarded the development of sex morality in the native girl. He replied in almost the identical language of the southern woman:

"I feel the most I can say is that we have succeeded in making the girls feel really that it is respectable to be married before their babies are born."

After returning from Hawaii the plan of undertaking welfare work for a corporation having branches in many parts of the United States was contemplated by the investigator. During a visit to their manufacturing plant in a small Pennsylvania community, made up of Pennsylvania Dutch, Hungarians, Slavs, etc., where a settlement house had been established, the problems of the community were discussed with the head worker and she was asked how she viewed the problem of sex relations. She made the following interesting reply:

"On the whole, I think the girls we have reached are coming to feel that it is respectable to be married before their babies are born."

Until Mr. Abraham Flexner's report on Prostitution in Europe was published, few people realized that the bulk of prostitutes have not "gone wrong," but that their mode of life is the outcome of the social concept of sex morality of the class from which they come. The development of the institution of marriage must be studied before one condemns as "immoral" the practices of a group whose morality is not yet removed from the "right of the seigneur" so universally recognized in all feudal states and which the colored races have had less opportunity to outgrow than any other peoples. The reproach that a colored woman is proud to bear a child by a white man can be surely traced back to the teaching in the tribes that it was an honor to bear a child by a chief. The very large percentage of colored people who have reached the higher concept of sex relations and marriage should form a strong basis on which to build hope for success in the education of the masses of this people along similar lines.

A number of people who are familiar with the history of the colored race in the United States and who know intimately the conditions under which they have lived, feel that it is an inconceivable injustice to measure their standards of sex morality by those of the white race. Mr. Joel E. Spingarn, Chairman of the Board of Directors of the National Association for the Advancement of Colored People said:

"There is nothing, in the first place, to show that sex immorality is not quite as grave a problem among white as it is among colored girls under sixteen years of age. Aside from this, however, we must take into consideration the fact that the colored people have little reason to believe in the sincerity of the sex morality professed by the white race. They have borne a heavy burden of the white man's lust which broke down the conceptions of morality, crude as they were, existing among the savage tribes from which the slaves were recruited. For this reason the deterrent public opinion, which among white people plays so prominent a part in maintaining the moral standards of white women as far as sex relations are concerned, has been of slower growth and is less harsh among the colored people. A colored girl's character is, therefore, more solidly based on inherent traits; that is, whether she 'goes wrong' or remains pure, she is more apt to do so because it is her nature to, than because of any pressure of public opinion brought to bear from outside. If that pressure were removed from white women, it might then, under all the circumstances, be interesting to discuss the relative sex morality of white and colored girls."

The members of this race, or mixture of races, whose destinies have been dominated always by the drop of Negro blood when that drop manifests itself in outward characteristics, must be helped up to the measure of older races by means that appeal to their own aspirations, likings and strivings.

There is a very general feeling both in the schools and among the social workers and colored clergymen, that the colored people themselves are developing rapidly and that conditions everywhere are growing better for them because of an increasingly wider knowledge of the race's accomplishment on the one hand, and of the growing need among themselves, on the other hand, for all manner of workers,—artisans, trades people and professional men and women. One of their educators in a recent address said:

"We who want to build and build firmly the foundations of a racial economy, believe that the vocation of a man in a modern civilized land includes not only the technique of his actual work, but intelligent comprehension of his elementary duties as a father, citizen and maker of public opinion, as a possible voter, a conserver of public health, an intelligent follower of moral customs, and one who can at least appreciate if not partake something of the higher spiritual life of the world. We do not believe that all these can be taught each individual in school, but it can be put into his social environment, and the more that environment is restricted and curtailed, the more emphatic is the demand that some part at least of the group shall be trained thoroughly in these higher matters of human development, if, and here is the crucial question, they are going to be able to share the surrounding civilization."

It must be reiterated again and again that this is the world's child race with a portion of its members grown to maturity, one might say, by hot house forcing, as opposed to the slow development of other civilized races. These maturer members of the race, in turning to give a helping hand to their slower, less fortunate brothers, must have the help of the older nations who have marched on before.

In one of Miss Lucy Pratt's wonderful "Ezekiel" stories, published in McClure's magazine, "The Little Number Ones," Ezekiel turns back from his place in the anniversary procession of the pupils of the colored school—the procession "moving ahead too, straight down between the lines, just as the others had done before,"—to aid the two little struggling twins, "the li'l number ones," to secure a place in the procession. Their small legs fail and both they and Ezekiel seem doomed to disappointment. But "Miss Lavinia," the wise white principal of the school, halts the marching column until the exhausted little figures are once more able to resume their way and join the others.

Her sister says, "'I'm glad you lent a helping hand just then.' 'Helping hand?' repeated the other vaguely. 'Helping hand,' she whispered. What was it about that and a race of children? She tried to recall, but Ezekiel's face seemed to be burning hauntingly up at her, filled with passionate reproach. 'I say dey's li'l number ones!' came his hoarse, despairing little shout again, 'You's 'blige ter help 'em! Dey's li'l number ones!'

"She could hear it again very plainly, that hoarse, despairing little shout, and very clearly she could see him coming again helping the faltering little figures over the rough and stony way that stretched out so hopelessly before them, encouraging them with soft, gasping whispers, as they slipped and stumbled by his side—and then, with their hands still held in his, still leading them on down the long, hard road, where the tramping procession had swept proudly ahead, and the better marchers had gone on before."

Name	Age	Sex	Grade	Marks		Teacher's Estimate		Reasons for port
				Con-duct	Work	Conduct	Mentality	
1. L. D.	15.4	f.	6A	B.	B.	Dignified.	Fair.	Irregular attendance.
2. G. B.	12.7	f.	6A	B.	B.	Excellent.	Poor.	Irregular atte dance, false hoods.
3. W. S.	12.7	f.	6A	A.	B.	Excellent.	Fair.	Irregular att dance; pov ty.
4. M. B.	13.4	f.	5E	C.	B.	Bad.	Good.	Misconduct.
5. R. S.	9.	m.	3A	B.	B.	Good.	Poor.	Poor attenti to studies.

Findings	Action Taken	Result	Remarks
immorality; ineffi- ent mother.	Ref. to S. P. C. C.; later to Settlement.	Nil; still at large and unregenerate.	S. P. C. C. said could not find sufficient evidence on which to convict; Settlement did not succeed in securing hold on girl.
falsehood, but mis- derstanding; belongs a Settlement club. rl slightly defective. mother.	Called attention of Settlement to case.	Seems more interested.	Child has no care whatever; is inclined to be silent, and lack of companionship at home aggravates this.
erty and poor home nditions; mother rking; no father.	Ref. to Social agency.	No improvement.	Case not followed up; principal difficulty in family two small children to be cared for.
immorality; no fath- mother working.	Ref. to S. P. C. C.	Sent to Hudson Tr. Sch.	Case of needed authority; grandmother reared child and had her always with her but became ill and child's mother, who was a domestic, could not care for her; was released by S. P. C. C. once before, after confessing to misconduct, and returned to school principal's care; volunteer supervision provided by Social agency but not followed up.
ed too much; sus- ted feebleminded- s; defective teeth breathing; both pa- ts working.	Recommended stricter discipline at home and mental examination at school.	Transferred to ungraded class temporarily.	The boy was nervous and jerky, and could not concentrate his attention upon anything; both parents work and he has little attention.

THIRTY-EIGHT CASES FROM THE "DIF

Name	Age	Sex	Grade	Marks		Teacher's Estimate		Reasons for port
				Con-duct	Work	Conduct	Mentality	
6. S. S.	8.3	f.	1A	C.	C.	Trouble-some.	Poor.	Suspected f ble minde ness.
7. A. B.	13.10	f.	7B	A.	B.	Mischievous.	Fair.	Truancy a general bad fluence.
8. L. H.	15.2	f.	7B	B.	B.	Wild.	Bright but lazy.	Left school wi out worki papers. S pected of bei wild.
9. N. W.	13.	f.	7B	B+	C.	Unruly.	Bright.	Truancy and regular atte dance.
10. L. R.	12.2	f.	3B	B.	C.	Trouble-some.	Poor.	Sex immoralit (One of gro of seven tected by pr cipal.)
11. C. T.	13.2	m.	6A	B.	B.	Good.	Bright.	Sex immoralit (One of gro of seven tected by p cipal.)

Findings	Action Taken	Result	Remarks
⌐ective eyesight and ⌐rvousness; grand-other took child away ⌐m widowed father; ⌐d home surroundings.	Recommended glasses, and placement in other custody, to visitor from Social agency.	Placed in ungraded class; no glasses supplied; no further action taken.	Probably the child should have had a chance in the regular grade after having been supplied with glasses, before being placed in an ungraded class.
⌐ immorality and il-⌐gal employment; lack ⌐ discipline at home; ⌐e on top floor of tene-⌐ent; mother rheuma-⌐ and illiterate; coun-⌐y bred; no father; be-⌐ged to evening ⌐sses.	Ref. to S. P. C. C. and Child Labor Committee.	Laundry proprietress warned; sent to uncle in Md. by S. P. C. C.	Mother was glad to have girl sent south; says the city is no place for girls.
⌐ difficulty about birth ⌐rtificate and could not ⌐derstand; did not like ⌐ool; good home, nice ⌐l.	Referred case to Board of Health and Census Bureau; straightened out case.	Working as dressmakers' apprentice.	
⌐t home to care for ⌐unger children and ⌐es not like school; ⌐nts to go to work.	Saw mother and referred her to a visitor who promised to call.	Nothing.	Has been a member of the Henrietta School evening classes for several years.
⌐ immorality; girl pal-⌐bly feebleminded and ⌐generate; mother and her both at work; ⌐ther low grade; girl ⌐d invited boys into ⌐ when alone; former-⌐in ungraded class but ⌐ently transferred.	Urged parents to have girl committed.	Parents refused to consent to commitment as L. is the only child; mother decided not to go to work any more; principal to have girl recommitted to ungraded class.	Principal requested that case should not be reported to S. P. C. C. This probably a mistake, as girl is a menace to companions.
⌐ immorality; said ⌐R. invited him into ⌐ and later with 2 ⌐er boys and 3 girls ⌐nt to basement in flat ⌐se.	Visited home; talked with boy and mother; referred cases to Settlement for visiting.	None; so far as could be learned; Settlement did not visit; no further complaint at school.	Boy seemed bright and normal; very much ashamed and seemed impressed with probable bad effects in later life if practice continued.

| Name | Age | Sex | Grade | Marks | | Teacher's Estimate | | Reasons for port |
				Con-duct	Work	Conduct	Mentality	
12. R. W.	15.2	f.	8B	B.	B.	Good and docile.	Average not good.	Cardiac trou and aunt tended plac her at work factory.
13. C. R.	14.4	f.	6B	C.	C.	Very bad.	Fairly bright	Sex immoral
14. A. J.	14.	f.	6B	B.	B.	Indifferent.	Fairly good.	Sex immorali
15. I. M.	15.1	f.	7A	C.	C.	Annoying.	Poor.	Intractability and questio able conduc
16. J. C.	16.	f.	5B	B.	C.	Fair.	Fair.	Intractability

Findings	Action Taken	Result	Remarks
Aunt stated factory where she herself worked (straw hats), safer than office for girl as attractive as R.; not sufficiently bright to teach.	Explained to aunt danger of placing girl with heart trouble at work on power machine.	Aunt consented to allow R. to attend night high school to learn stenography.	Aunt makes $35 a week in season (Dec. to May) working at straw hats; has been with same firm 15 years; earns enough to live on for balance of year; has elevator apt. and keeps lodgers.
Girl bad; accused of taking earnings of other girl from prostitution and of making appointments with men for other girl; both parents working; did not know of girl's doings.	Took to S. P. C. C. for prosecution.	Committed to Hudson, June 4, 1913.	Seemingly a vicious character.
f. C. R.; both parents working; girl had no care.	Same as C. R.	cf. C. R.	These two girls, although totally unrelated, have about the same physique, and the same mental and moral characteristics.
Bad home influence; girl weak and silly.	Ref. to social agency.	Understand that nothing was done. School nurse had her committed to Hudson 4 mos. later.	This is a degenerate family. After learning facts about mother and girl, boy was examined and found feebleminded. Under care of volunteer supervisor from social agency.
No parents; does not like uncle with whom she lives; says he overworks her in his laundry.	Ref. to visitor from social agency.	Visitor kept in touch with girl; did not recommend her for employment.	No improvement; left school and went to work as housemaid; kept same place 5 mos. (was still there at last accounts).

Name	Age	Sex	Grade	Marks		Teacher's Estimate		Reasons for port
				Con-duct	Work	Conduct	Mentality	
17. C. W.	16.5	m.	6B	B-C	B-C	Overbearing	Special kind	Over-age. Should work
18. W. L.	10.1	m.	5A	B.	B.	Good.	Good qual-ity.	Truancy.
19. W. K.	11.6	m.	5E	B.	C.	Trouble-some.	Sluggish.	Truancy and falsifying.
20. G. M.	9.4	f.	2B	D.	B.	Very good.	Doubtful.	Poor attendan
21. J. E.	10.5	m.	4B	C.	C.	Trouble-some.	Good.	Truancy and misconduct.

⌐T CHILDREN" GROUP—(Continued)

Findings	Action Taken	Result	Remarks
⌐ther dead; mother ⌐orks hard to give boy ⌐pportunity to become ⌐usician; boy works as ⌐borer to earn money ⌐r lessons and to get ⌐othes.	Ref. to visitor from social agency.	Employment as office boy given; had to answer telephone and use complicated filing system; incompetent; returned to school and refused to leave.	Understand visitor did not have musical talent tested, because boy refused to go to music school settlement. Said he preferred his regular teacher. Appeared to be a case of misfit position.
⌐ther dead; mother a ⌐omestic; has never ⌐ken care of boy, but ⌐as a furnished room in ⌐hich both live; mother ⌐as no sense of responsibility; boy is shy with ⌐ttle power of self-expression; needs companionship.	Ref. to colored church for Boy Scouts but this did not hold him.	Boy sent to Juvenile Asylum.	Boy might have been placed in another home or boarded; his mother could have paid a part of his maintenance; as a rule far better plan than asylum.
⌐s never been disciplined at home; father a ⌐ailroad employee and ⌐rinks; mother works ⌐ shirtwaist factory; ⌐oy runs about at will ⌐xcept such care as he ⌐eceives at day nursery.	Asked mother if she could not place him for day with some friend who was a good disciplinarian. She said they were going to send him to boarding-school next year. Ref. to social agency for volunteer supervision.	None; boy still at school; still truant and delinquent.	Boy should go to parental school; recommended this to principal.
⌐ild kept at home to ⌐are for infant of guardian.	Took to dispensary. Ref. to social agency for sustained treatment.	Nothing done; family moved away.	Apparently neglected case.
⌐and brother deserted ⌐y mother; both illegitimate and cared for by ⌐randmother who supports them and her ⌐other by going out to ⌐ay's work; has father's ⌐ddress but he has never ⌐ontributed to boys' ⌐upport; mother has ⌐isappeared; grandmother fine, energetic ⌐ersonality; says often ⌐hey have nothing but ⌐read to eat.	Ref. to C. O. S. for aid. Later ref. to social agency who placed boy under volunteer supervision.	Washing given by C. O. S.; at end of investigation boy's conduct and work marks had dropped to D.	

Name	Age	Sex	Grade	Marks		Teacher's Estimate		Reasons for port
				Con-duct	Work	Conduct	Mentality	
22. M. B.	15.4	f.	Ung.	B.	D.	Good.	None.	Asked to b committed Randall's and.
23. M. R.	10.6	f.	3A	B.	B.	Fair.	Fair.	Bad attenda
24. S. R.	9.2	f.	3B	A.	C.	Fair.	Fair.	Bad attenda
25. W. M.	10.2	m.	3B	B.	B.	Surly and cross.	Unsatisfac-tory.	Truancy.
26. E. W.	13.6	m.	D.	B.	B.	Fair.	Slow.	Need for re ation (Re ported by tendance ficer).
27. J. H.	7.11	m.	2B	B.	B.	Good.	Fair.	Truancy.

Findings	Action Taken	Result	Remarks
...en to Dr. Schlapp's ...nic where she was ad-...dged a low grade im-...cile.	Committed to Randall's Island.	Still there; happy and contented; mother much relieved.	Mother who goes out to day's work has somewhat abnormal personality; brother is also slightly below par mentally.
...gular home arrange-...ents; girl and sister ...pt home alternately ...care for infant broth-...; father deserted ...mily; mother help-...ss but nice woman.	Ref. to social agency to find mother employment, secure relief and place baby in day nursery. Recommended that older children be committed to institution.	Clothing furnished children; unsuccessful effort to secure employment for mother; now in a home for consumptives. Baby dead.	Example of fatal consequences which failure to make connections and do persistent follow-up work sometimes has.
...ee No. 23.	See No. 23.	Child is on the street, neglected, because nothing final was done to help the family.	
... and brother living ...th aunt and grand-...other, both of whom ...out to day's work; ...ther sees boys only ...ce a month; W. chron-...truant with no one ...care for him; case ...eviously referred to ...cial agency by school; ...results.	Called case to attention of social agency visitor and had W. tested by field worker of Public Education Ass'n for mentality.	Found under-age mentally. Volunteer visitor supervised boy and reported improvement; school record shows decline to C. in both work and deportment.	This case previously referred to the same social agency. Notes of their visitor on case show supervisor appointed who reported progress; younger boy nice child but sadly neglected.
...nd boy working for ...ocer who said he was ...o busy for a club; ...ly has time for Sun-...y School, and occasionally "movies."	Reported back to attendance officer.	None.	Boy seemed to enjoy work; did not urge anything further.
...nd irregular home ...e; mother was nurse ...West Indies and never ...d the care of her own ...ildren until they were ...own; mother nice ...oman but inefficient; ...control over the chil-...en; boy suffers with ...se bleed.	Talked with mother about children's future and her responsibility; told her of S. P. C. C. commitment for improper guardianship; reported physical condition to school nurse. Ref. to social agency for supervision.	Mother working at home taking in laundry instead of going out to day's work; moved to another neighborhood and took boarders. Boy's attendance improving.	

Name	Age	Sex	Grade	Marks		Teacher's Estimate		Reasons for port
				Con-duct	Work	Conduct	Mentality	
28. B.McK.	12.2	f.	Ung.	B.	B.	Very bad.	Low.	Bad influenc class. Mar tendency t improper a tions wher with boys.
29. E. W.	14.7	m.	Ung.	A.	B.	Two teachers gave diametrically opposed opinions. One said boy was vicious and should be removed from school; the other said his conduct was excellent; that he had a good mind and was a good influence.		Institutional commitmer desired for boy.
30. M. F.	13.	m.	Ung.	C.	D.	Doing well now.	Very low.	Asked to ha him commit to institut for feeble-minded.
31. O. C.	8.	m.	3A	B.	C.	Fair.	Unable to judge because of ill health.	Reported as berculous.

т Children" Group—(Continued)

Findings	Action Taken	Result	Remarks
...nd home conditions ...ry bad; house dirty; children of different ...lor; suggestive pic...res on wall; girl a waif, ...d no known relatives; ...inted swelling under ...in that has had no ...re.	Recommended for institutional care. Wrote inspector of ungraded classes advising that S. P. C. C. be asked to commit for improper guardianship.	Nothing done; girl still at school irregularly.	
... has no control at ...me; father does not ...e with mother and other goes out to day's ...rk; should go to an ...stitution.	Visited mother and aunt 4 times and pastor twice. Mother refused unqualifiedly to part with boy who is only child. Pastor thought boy's brains were "only addled" and that he would be all right as he grew older; promised to try to influence mother to commit boy after he was assured that boy was a moral and mental defective.	No result; boy still at school at close of investigation.	
... cataracts; never ...en able to see plainly; ...ungest of 12 children; ...tends Catholic Sun...y School where priest ...charge says he is one ...his most helpful boys.	Advised mother to take to eye and ear hospital for treatment of cataracts and recommended that boy be transferred to school with classes for blind.	Transfer to blind class secured for boy through field worker of Public Education Ass'n.	Commitment to institution for feebleminded had been recommended for boy by previous visitor.
...ily conditions very ...or; father and mother ...norant, illiterate south...n negroes just moved ...New York; furniture ...apidated and house ...tidy; evidences of ...eat poverty.	Case had previously been referred to social agency by the school without any result. Advised with visitor regarding clinical treatment for boy.	Boy given clinical treatment and taken out of school, later placed in hospital where he was trephined; after return to school threatened to commit suicide by jumping out of window in clerk's office; after this vounteer visitor was appointed.	In view of home conditions, visitor from agency was urged to push case for institutional commitment through S.P.C.C. if necessary.

| Name | Age | Sex | Grade | Marks | | Teacher's Estimate | | Reasons for port |
				Con-duct	Work	Conduct	Mentality	
32. T. H.	14.	m.	Ung.	B.	B.	Very good.	Very quick.	Head of depa ment f should lea school a work.
33. F. M.	12.6	m.	4A	A.	C.	Excellent.	Has brains if he would only use them.	In connection with immor ity charges against a m who had i moral relatio with F. an other schoo boys.
34. C. M.	12.1	m.	E5	B.	C.	Very trouble-some.	Deficient.	Chronic tru-ancy.

ᴛ CHILDREN" GROUP—*(Continued)*

Findings	Action Taken	Result	Remarks
ᴏther away from home; ᴏy living in basement ᴏoms with father who ᴠas janitor; one of boy's ᴇgs considerably shorter ᴛhan other and marked ᴎpediment in his speech. Physician in ungraded ᴅept. of Bd. of Educaᴛion stated boy should ᴀave special eye examiᴀation, but as school ᴀhysician did not examᴎe ungraded pupils, ᴏothing had been done ᴀbout this.)	Took boy to German clinic for examination and found he had orthopedic defect and chorea; Dr. prescribed brace and hospital furnished same. Boy refused to wear brace because he could not play baseball in it. Warned father of serious results to boy's future health if not properly attended to. Referred to pastor of a colored Church for visiting.	Nothing appreciable; when investigation closed, boy still playing in street without brace; never visited so far as could be learned.	This boy is such a physical wreck little could be accomplished; Dr. Fisk of the German clinic said that sooner or later he would become bed-ridden.
ᴠry bad home influence; ᴀther not living at ᴏme; never married to ᴎother; sister commitᴇd to Hudson Training ᴄhool for sex immorᴀlity.	Boy was examined and found positively feebleminded; measured 9 years mentally. Mother refused to have him committed to institution; says he is no worse than other boys. Ref. to social agency for sustained attention. Boy placed in charge of volunteer visitor.	Nothing appreciable.	Nothing short of institution and regulation of living régime would seem to have any effect on this case.
ᴠry bad home conditions; indications of ᴦreat poverty; had nevᴇr been to school until ᴦ0½ yrs. old with exᴄeption of 6 mos. in 7th ᴠear; father had been ᴦruck gardener in Florᴅa and boy kept out of ᴄhool to aid him. Fathᴇr died in 1909 and ᴎother brought 2 boys ᴏ New York; she goes ᴏut to day's work as ᴀundress and is in poor ᴀealth; said he did not ᴠish to go to school beᴄause his teacher had ᴄtruck him over the ᴀead with a ruler while ᴀsleep in class after he ᴀad been up all night ᴠith sick mother; lodger ᴎ house confirmed story ᴏf mother's illness and ᴏoy's being up all night.	Referred matter of corporal punishment to Sec'y of Com. on Hyg. of School Children and later at her request to Supt. of Schools for investigation; nothing further heard from it. Told boy he was only injuring himself and future prospects by course and advised going back to school. Boy preferred to work and stated he had job at grocery store from 1:30 p. m. to 12 at $3.00 a week. Referred to social agency for follow-up work.	Boy still truant at close of investigation.	

| Name | Age | Sex | Grade | Marks | | Teacher's Estimate | | Reasons f port |
				Con-duct	Work	Conduct	Mentality	
35. J. G.	10.	m.	4B	A.	B.	Growing trouble-some.	Good.	Incipient ancy.
36. E. T.	12.6	f.	3A	B.	C.	Not bad but offensive personal-ity.	Very low.	Unusual a of absen

CHILDREN" GROUP—(*Continued*)

Findings	Action Taken	Result	Remarks
⌐ bad home condi-⌐ns; mother dead; her longshoreman ⌐h irregular hours but ⌐ing to keep house-⌐d together; one ⌐ther in truant school; ⌐er brother works in ⌐e store and does ⌐sework, cooking, etc.; ⌐use very dirty and ⌐k; boy sweet-man-⌐ed and has good mind ⌐ is unkempt.	Talked with father; recommended mov-ing to lighter apart-ment and hiring el-derly woman to do housework; father anxious to do best possible but unwilling to have woman stead-ily in house; says they make trouble. Reported case to so-cial agency.	Boy's father has him stay with aunt during day-time; for last term of investiga-tion boy's record shows no absence whatever; boy showed much bet-ter care.	This was the worst kept home, with one exception, found during the investigation. Six mice were counted running about during visit.
⌐e conditions poor; her dead; mother out ⌐ day's work; home ⌐an but poorly fur-⌐hed; S. P. C. C. have ⌐ord of mother living ⌐h her brother-in-law ⌐o also had improper ⌐ations with girl; ⌐ther said E.'s absence ⌐e to nasal hemor-⌐age, making hospital ⌐atment necessary.	Took E. to hospital and examining doc-tor secured state-ment from her that she had had improp-er relations with nu-merous men; found she was suffering from gonorrhea; took girl to S. P. C. C. at once who took her and two other girls implicated by her into custody.	All 3 girls sent to Hudson Training School but no criminal proceed-ings instituted against men al-though several were named; S. P. C. C. states "in prosecutions of this character the credibility of the complaining wit-ness is of para-mount import-ance;" in this con-nection S. P. C. C.'s attention was called to the fact that one of the men named by E. had been report-ed to the investi-gator by a school principal for simi-lar offenses	

THIRTY-EIGHT CASES FROM THE "Di

| Name | Age | Sex | Grade | Marks | | Teacher's Estimate | | Reasons for port |
				Conduct	Work	Conduct	Mentality	
37.L.McC.	14.8	m.	4B	B.	B.	Good.	Good.	Employment after schoo without wo ing papers.
38. W. S.	12.	m.	4A	B	B.	Good.	Slow.	Much absen and need clothing.

171

Findings	Action Taken	Result	Remarks
ellent home condi-ns; mother and andmother both in-ligent and working home as laundress d hair-worker, mak-g a combined income $18–$20 a week; y's father had died en he was 3 yrs. old; nily living in New rk only 6 mos., com-g here from North rolina; mother said y worked at moving ture theatre turning n reel, working from 0–10 p. m. week-ys and to 12 p. m., urdays and Sundays; id $3.00 a week.	Referred to Child La-bor Committee.	Child Labor Com. report no offense against child la-bor laws found.	The attendance of-ficer at the school said that this moving picture theatre was a flagrant offender against the child labor law, many of the school boys working there suc-cessively.
nd boy living with nt and kept home fre-ently to care for in-t of aunt; father liv-g with daughter at other address; boy gged in the extreme, ked thin and badly red for.	Reported case to S. P. C. C. for action on score of improper guardianship. S. P. C. C. at first found nothing wrong with home conditions, but later persuaded fath-er to take boy to live with him in home of married sister.	Boy's attendance is regular and he was well-dressed and looked happy and contented when seen during last part of the inves-tigation.	

APPENDIX II

DIRECTORY OF SOCIAL AGENCIES FOR COLORED PEOPLE

This report includes all the secular agencies, and four churches which are typical of the institutional work done by the colored churches.   Dec., 1913.

National Association for the Advancement of Colored People, Inc., 70 Fifth Ave., New York city.

SECRETARY.—Miss May Childs Nierney.

BOARD OF DIRECTORS.—White and colored.

WORKERS.—White and colored.

Makes propaganda by means of meetings, etc., against race discrimination of whatsoever nature.

Publishes "The Crisis," W. E. B. Dubois, Editor, a monthly magazine devoted to race topics.

Conducts a continuous campaign against lynching, segregation, etc.

National League on Urban Conditions among Negroes, 127 West 135th Street, New York city.

George Edmund Hayes, Ph.D., Field Secretary: Eugene Kinckle Jones, M.A., Asst. Field Secretary.

BOARD OF DIRECTORS.—White and colored.

WORKERS.—Colored.

WORK.—For colored people only.

Travelers' Aid to colored women.

Women's club, meeting at Free Kindergarten Association.

Boys' club, meeting at N. Y. Colored Mission and White Rose Industrial Home.

School Visitor.

Big Brothers (colored).

Big Sisters (colored).

Employment bureau.

Boys' summer camp.

Investigation of housing conditions.

Promotes conference of workers among colored girls.

New York Colored Mission, 225–227 West 30th St., New York city.

HEADWORKER.—Miss Peffer.

BOARD OF DIRECTORS.—All white.

WORKERS.—White and colored.

WORK.—For colored people only—non-sectarian.

Day nursery, capacity 23 babies.   Trained nurse in charge.   Fee 5 cents per day.   (Older children have free play in back yard after school.)

Boys' club, carpentry class and athletics.

Girls' afternoon sewing class and evening embroidery class.

Men Mechanics,' Elevator Men's and Public Porters' Association, under auspices of National League on Urban Conditions among Negroes.

Music classes.

Employment bureau, domestic help.

Lodging house for women.

Social evening, Friday.

Sunday evening religious meeting for young people.

Church of St. Benedict the Moor, Catholic, West 53rd St., New York city.

PASTOR.—Father Thomas M. O'Keefe.

Sunday School.

Young men's and young women's societies.

Flat with living quarters for unemployed girls.

Employment bureau.

Men's and women's church organizations.

(This church, together with St. Mark's Chapel in Harlem, represents the Catholic mission work among colored people in New York, dealing with relief, unemployment and the social problems.)

St. Cyprian's Parish House, 177 West 63rd St., New York city.

PASTOR.—Rev. Joseph W. Johnson.

Gymnasium.

Needlework Guild.—Employs women and girls of the neighborhood, paying them from 5 cents to 20 cents an hour for plain sewing; garments sold to neighborhood people at cost.

Laundry.—Employs neighborhood women; all handwork and open air drying.

Model flat.

Cooking and housekeeping classes.

Milk station.

Women's club.

Girls' clubs.

B ys' clubs.

Fresh air work.

Employment bureau.

Friendly visiting.

Deaconess of Episcopal church mission together with Mrs. Johnson, wife of pastor, in charge of social work.

Henrietta Industrial School (Children's Aid Society), 224 West 63rd St., New York city.

PRINCIPAL.—Miss M. L. Stewart.

BOARD OF DIRECTORS AND MANAGEMENT.—White.

WORKERS.—White.

Four hundred and sixty-five colored children enrolled in Public School grades 1-A—4-B.

Day Classes.—Sewing, cooking, carpentry, cobbling and basket work.

Evening Classes.—Elementary, home and restaurant cooking. Elementary and advanced dressmaking.

Boys' club.

Girls' model flat—living room, kitchen, bedroom, bath-room—open five nights a week.

Friendly visiting.

Free Kindergarten Association for Colored Children, 202 West 63rd St., New York city.

HEADWORKER.—Miss Helen Titus Emerson.

BOARD OF DIRECTORS.—White and colored.

Kindergarten.
Library.
Penny provident fund.
Branch of Music School Settlement.
Senior and junior boys' clubs—hand work and games.
Senior and junior girls' clubs—housekeeping, dancing, singing, doll's clothes and games.
Mothers' meetings.
Mothers' club.
Amusement club of National League on Urban Conditions among Negroes.
Summer school and play center.
Outings, theatre parties, etc.
Home visiting.

Lincoln Day Nursery,* 202 West 63rd St., New York city.
SUPERINTENDENT.—Mrs. S. Green.
BOARD OF DIRECTORS.—White.
WORKERS.—Colored.
WORK.—For colored people only.
CAPACITY.—79 children—40 babies.
Older children cared for after school by Free Kindergarten Association for Colored Children in same building.
Children from Day Nursery graduate into kindergarten.
Mothers' club meets once a month.
Summer home at Mt. Kisco, on ten acres of land given by friend of the Day Nursery at nominal rent; maintained by Day Nursery.

Stillman House, Branch of Henry Street Settlement,† 205 West 60th St., New York city.
DIRECTION OF—Henry Street Settlement (white).
HEADWORKER.—Miss Ida Morgan.
WORKERS.—White and colored.
WORK.—For both white and colored people.
Seven trained nurses.
Study hours for school children.
Play room open after school.
Penny provident fund.
Branch of public library.

Men's club
Mothers' club } Actively interested in neighborhood affairs. Thanks-
Parents' club   giving and Christmas parties given for the poor.

Uncle Remus clubs, No. 1 and No. 2, reproducing and acting Uncle Remus stories, and giving instruction in raffia and basketry.
City History club for children.
Dramatic club for girls.
Carpentry classes for boys.
Athletic clubs for boys.

* This has been discontinued and the house is occupied by the colored branch of the Henry Street Settlement, which is now called Lincoln House. The activities of the Settlement are much the same as those formerly conducted at Stillman House. (See Stillman House.)
† Now called Lincoln House. See Lincoln Day Nursery.

Cooking classes for girls (cooking teacher supplied by University Extension Society, which pays half her salary. Settlement pays other half).

Dancing class.

Manicuring and shampooing class for women.

Number reached by clubs and classes, about 500 a week.

Fresh air work, boys go to Settlement Camp Henry. Mothers and babies go to Settlement farm at Montclair. Girls go to P. E. Church home at White Plains.

Summer playground, equipped by Parks and Playgrounds Department of city. Worker supplied by Settlement. Average weekly attendance 473.

West End Workers' Association.

HEADQUARTERS.—Lincoln House, 202 West 63rd St., New York city.

SECRETARY.—Miss Ida Morgan.

PROGRAM FOR YEAR.—To improve police conditions on San Juan Hill.

Nov. 1914.

SECRETARY.—Miss H. T. Emerson.

PROGRAM FOR YEAR.—To better tenement conditions in same neighborhood.

White Rose Industrial Association, 217 East 86th St., New York city.

SUPERINTENDENT.—Mrs. J. E. Farrell.

BOARD OF DIRECTORS.—White and colored.

WORKERS.—Colored.

WORK.—For colored people only.

Lodging home for working girls. Co-operates with Travelers' Aid visitor of National League on Urban Conditions among Negroes.

Sewing classes for children.

Cobbling class for boys.

Boys' club.

Cooking instruction given to girls who have lodged in home and afterward become housemaids.

Religious service Sunday.

Young Women's Christian Association, 121 West 132nd St., New York city.

BOARD OF DIRECTORS.—Colored.

WORKERS.—Colored.

WORK.—For colored people only.

Lodging accommodations for 20 young women—no meals served.

Classes in embroidery, dressmaking, stenography, cooking, vocal music, Bible study and physical culture.

Camp Fire Girls' circle.

Basket ball and tennis court on grounds.

Employment bureau.

Library.

The Young Men's Christian Association was not included, as at the time of the investigation it was not doing any distinctive work with colored boys.

Hope Day Nursery, Incorporated, 123 West 133rd St., New York city.

BOARD OF DIRECTORS.—Colored.

WORKERS.—Colored.

WORK.—For colored children only.

MATRON.—On vacation; Board of Managers in charge.

Forty-five children can be accommodated.

Mothers' club in process of organization.

Older children of working mothers cared for after school but no organized activities are maintained for them.

St. Philip's Institutional Church (Protestant Episcopal), 215 West 133rd St., New York City.

PASTOR.—Rev. Hutchins C. Bishop.

PASTOR'S ASSISTANT (in charge of social activities).—Rev. I. W. Daniels.

Sunday school.

Senior and junior clubs for boys and girls.

Boy Scouts.

Gymnasium.

Sewing classes for children.

Men's and women's church guilds.

Home for the aged.

Salem Methodist Episcopal Church (Institutional), 104 West 133rd St., New York City.

PASTOR.—Rev. W. E. Cullen.

Sunday school.

Clubs for boys and girls.

Gymnasium.

Boy Scouts.

Church societies for men and women.

St. John's House for Working Girls, 36 West 134th St., New York City.

SUPERINTENDENT.—Mrs. M. B. Gregory.

SUPPORTED BY—Women's Auxiliary of the Cathedral of St. John the Divine.

Provides living accommodations for working women and girls (not including board).

Women's clubs.

Boys' and girls' clubs.

Boy Scouts.

Sewing classes for children.

Chair-caning and cobblery classes for boys.

(A clinic attended by a colored physician was about to be established at the time the investigation closed.)

Note: Since the close of the investigation, this Home has removed to West 131st St.

Music School Settlement for Colored People, 257 West 134th St., New York city.

MUSICAL DIRECTOR.—Mr. David I. Martin.

BRANCH.—202 West 63rd St., New York city.

INSTRUCTION in piano, violin, voice culture, sight singing and theory, 'cello.

Three hundred and thirty-two pupils registered in all departments.

Senior orchestra.

Childrens' orchestra.

Milk Station of Babies' Welfare Association, 36 West 139th St., New York city.

In addition to milk station activities (weighing babies, selling various grades of milk, etc.) a mothers' club has recently been organized.